# Saving Psychotherapy:
## How therapists can bring the talking cure back from the brink

# Saving Psychotherapy:
## How therapists can bring the talking cure back from the brink

**Benjamin E. Caldwell, PsyD**

First Printing: 2015

Typeset in Times New Roman 11 pt and Avenir

ISBN-13: 978-0-9888759-6-8
ISBN-10: 0-9888759-6-9

Benjamin E. Caldwell
6222 Wilshire Blvd, Suite 200
Los Angeles, CA 90048

www.bencaldwell.com

Ordering Information:

Discounts are available on quantity purchases by educators, corporations, associations, and others. For details, contact the publisher at the above listed address.

U.S. trade bookstores and wholesalers: Please contact Benjamin E. Caldwell, 323-246-8823, or email ben@bencaldwell.com.

*To those who show up*
*and care*
*and are ready*
*to stand up*

# Contents

# Acknowledgements

Inevitably I will leave out some people who have been quite helpful in the development and delivery of the ideas contained here. Please know that this section does not define the boundaries of my gratitude.

My thanks to my current professional home, Alliant International University, for giving me the sabbatical that allowed this project to reach fruition. From the time I began my graduate study at what was then United States International University (the name changed after a merger with the California School of Professional Psychology), Alliant has supported and nurtured my career.

As it relates specifically to this book, Angela Kahn has seen more drafts than a haunted house. More drafts than a beer factory. More drafts than a fantasy football power player. More drafts than any reasonable person could have been expected to read. And each time she came through with patience, encouragement, and insight.

Few writers are lucky enough to call their editor "Dad," and I'm humbled and grateful for the privilege. Chris Caldwell made more and better change than the Franklin Mint. He often was able to translate my idea word casserole into something resembling understandable English. He was also encouraging at every turn.

Scott Woolley, Diane Gehart, Olivia Loewy, and Aimee Clark are all very skilled educators and therapists, and were all kind enough to read early drafts and offer the benefit of their wisdom. Each one made the end result much better.

It is no secret that we stand on the shoulders of giants in the field of psychotherapy, and this book is no different. I owe an intellectual debt to Bruce Wampold, Barry Duncan, Scott Miller, Louis Cozolino, Dan Siegel, my friend and colleague Sean Davis, and many others. You'll see here that I often summarize their work in service of a particular argument I am making, but if the summary captures your interest, rest assured that a longer look at their work will be richly rewarding.

Finally, my fantastic interns at Caldwell-Clark have generously offered their time, discussion, and insight to the work you see here. As new professionals, they are undoubtedly among those who will be most impacted by the trends here, and they are most eager to take action. Gabrielle Moore, Jeff Liebert, Matthew Brinkley, and Claire Hapke, my thanks to each of you, and I hope this can help guide your next steps.

# Preface

The field of psychotherapy in the United States is in trouble. As I'll explain in the first section of this book, it has been for some time. Even before the economic recession of 2008-2010, public utilization of outpatient therapy was declining, and total spending on therapy (from all sources, public and private) was dropping precipitously. This trend has continued, and comes in spite of decades of very strong research data supporting the simple and inescapable solution that therapy works.

I'm not the first person to notice this. You could even argue that I'm late to the party, as others have been sounding the alarm for some time. Articles on the issue include:

- Psychotherapy's image problem (*New York Times*, 2013)
- The trouble with talk therapy (*Time*, 2012)
- Where has all the psychotherapy gone? (APA's *Monitor on Psychology*, 2010)
- The decline of psychotherapy (*Psychiatric Times*, 2008)
- Is therapy dead? (*Salon*, 2004)

These and other writings on the topic usually come with suggestions for what the field of psychotherapy can do to reverse its slide. Their calls have gone largely unheeded, though, and their warnings generally ignored. The authors of such pieces, many of whom are well-respected therapists themselves, have called for large-scale, collective efforts toward solutions. And for the most part, they have been met with silence.

I don't think the problem is that therapists don't care. Every therapist I know is heavily invested in the continued availability and success of psychotherapy, not just for themselves but for the communities they serve. The problem is that those sounding ominous warnings about the future or even the present-day status of psychotherapy *have called for large-scale, collective efforts* that most of us have little control over. Suggestions that we should pool our money for a television ad campaign, produce more applicable research, or generally make psychotherapy more science-based are simply out of the reach of most individual practitioners. For therapists who are merely trying to make a living while making a difference, we shrug our shoulders and hope that those in charge will help us out. The more rare suggestions of what we can do on an individual level have tended to focus on marketing and branding, which may make an individual therapist's practice more sustainable, but which have no impact on the larger problems in the field.

This book is an attempt to show how you as an individual therapist, acting on your own in ways that will improve your practice, can *also* help the field of psychotherapy as a whole. As I will explain, some collective efforts are necessary to fix what has gone wrong in the psychotherapy professions. But we also have the ability to take *immediate, individual actions* that will have both personal and collective benefit.

When it comes to warning therapists of the state of the psychotherapy field today, this book has few things to say that haven't been said elsewhere, though I hope you'll find the *way* the story is told here to be interesting and informative. It certainly is more inclusive in scope than most works on the topic, which have centered on a single professional group rather than encompassing all of the professionals impacted by psychotherapy's struggles.

What makes this book meaningfully different, I believe, is that it is more than a warning or a critique. It is *an action plan for the individual therapist*. It is an attempt to clarify how you can, through a number of relatively simple acts, raise the profile of psychotherapy and the respectability of psychotherapists in the eyes of your community. In doing so you can help the field change the course it is currently on, a course of becoming a marginalized profession largely by and for the wealthy. And you can make many of these changes no matter where you are in your career, from student to seasoned professional.

Of course, your choosing to take the steps I outline here is no guarantee that your colleagues will also do so. Again, this is where I believe this book differs from other commentaries and suggestions about salvaging our field from its current path. If enough psychotherapists play active, individual roles in improving the standing of our field, we can turn the proverbial ship. But even if we don't, the actions you take on an individual level can ensure that you are one of those – perhaps one of the few – whose practice survives and succeeds in spite of our collective slide.

I wrote this in hopes that it would help all of us. But I also wrote it to help *you, even if no one else changes a thing.*

# About me

You might understandably ask what qualifies me to make the claims and suggestions I'm making in this book. Unless you've had me as an instructor or seen me present at a conference, you probably haven't ever heard of me. And frankly, my own history isn't all that important. I hope the facts presented here speak for themselves, and that the conclusions drawn from them make good logical sense. But it might help you to know how I came to these conclusions.

I grew up in Kansas, and moved to San Diego in 1998 to begin a master's degree program in marriage and family therapy at what was then United States International University. I ultimately went on to complete my doctorate, and during that time, I fell in love with teaching. I finished my PsyD in late 2004 and was soon hired by the university to teach full-time in its undergraduate Psychology program.

The following year, the university – which by then had changed its name to Alliant International University as it merged with the California School of Professional Psychology, a name many veteran therapists will recognize – asked me to move to Sacramento to launch our family therapy program there. I accepted, and it was around the same time that I offered to join the Legislative and Advocacy Committee for the California Division of the American Association for Marriage and Family Therapy (AAMFT).

This may all sound like resume data so far, but that last part is important to how I wound up writing this book. When I joined the AAMFT-California advocacy group, *I didn't know anything about advocacy.* I wanted to be of service to our field, but I had no idea how. My colleagues in the Division didn't mind; I was going to be in Sacramento where I could connect with policymakers, and I cared about the work that therapists like me were doing. That was enough for them. They made me chair of the committee.

I remained in that role for most of the 10 years that followed. In that time, I worked on a number of major issues that shaped how I think about the professions: Experience requirements for MFT licensure, the launching of a counselor license in California, hiring policies in the Department of Corrections, California's first-in-the-nation ban on reparative therapy for minors, and many more. I spent a lot of time researching and acting on these issues, usually in collaboration with other mental health professional groups but occasionally in opposition to them.

That advocacy work has shaped me in more ways than I can describe. It also has given me a perspective on the mental health professions, and how the professions are governed, that I believe most therapists lack: I've seen the inner workings of a state licensing board, of legislative committees, of both sides of the accreditation process, and of appointed policymakers. I've built bridges across professions when it has been helpful to do so, and stood up to other professional groups when that was needed.

You might find such inner workings mundane. Believe me, I can tell when I'm going into too much detail in a policy discussion in one of my classes, because I can watch as students' eyes slowly glaze over. That's okay! This book is not going to be an endless set of notes of subcommittee discussions, I promise. I've found that kind of work fascinating, in no small part because it has shown me how the people who are making decisions about our professions actually think about the work we do. It also has taught me a lot about the complicated relationship between facts and politics.

I'm happy to report that this experience hasn't made me a cynic. As I hope you'll see in this text, it's done quite the opposite. As best as I can tell, every single policymaker or staff person with whom I have worked in the past 10 years has been genuinely trying to do what they believe is best for the community they serve. Of course, they have to balance what they think would be helpful with what they think is achievable; few of us want to be known as champions of lost causes. But I have been surprised, more times than I can count, by the power that one person has to make change. That one person doesn't need to be a lawyer or legislator or lobbyist. *You just need to show up, and you need to care.* That by itself can make a lot of things achievable.

Today, I am a licensed marriage and family therapist in Los Angeles, specializing in working with couples. I've been licensed for about 10 years, and if you include the work I did as a student and then as a graduate intern, I've been practicing for more than 15.

# Technicalities

There are a couple of things worth clarifying about how I use language in this book. First and foremost, I talk a great deal here about the psychotherapy "field" or "profession," knowing that what I'm actually referring to is a *family* of professions: Psychologists, professional counselors, clinical social workers, and family therapists are the main groups I talk about in this text. To be sure, those psychiatrists, nurses, pastoral counselors, addiction counselors, and others who perform psychotherapy are also part of the psychotherapy profession, even though they may not fit neatly into the categories defined by licensure. My intention is simply ease of reading, and not to leave anyone out who rightly belongs in. If you're a psychotherapist, in whatever form, then my discussion of the psychotherapy profession includes you. Any time I use collective terms like "we," "us," and "our," I mean all of us psychotherapists, except in those few instances where it's clear that I mean something more specific.

Throughout the book as a matter of convenience you'll see me refer to counselors as LPCs, social workers as LCSWs, and family therapists as LMFTs. The abbreviations can vary a bit depending on the formal license title where you are, so please know that my intention there isn't to be exclusionary, it's just shorthand. For example, if you're licensed as a *clinical* counselor as several states do, and thus use the title "LPCC" or "LCPC," I'm still including you when I say "LPC."

Secondly, you will see me give case examples on a few occasions here. While these examples draw from my clinical experience, the details are fictionalized to protect the confidentiality of my clients. Any similarity to real people is coincidental.

Finally, you will see endnotes used throughout this text. Much as I like APA style (really!), using in-text citations here would quickly get cumbersome to read. But I do want to make it clear where I got the factual statements included here, so endnotes seemed to be the best solution. Many of the facts in this book are not widely known, even though they are drawn from public or academic sources. I came to them through my experience as an advocate, through my academic work, and through exchanges with colleagues around the state and around the country.

If nothing else, the references in the endnotes should help distinguish between the statements that are established facts and those that are simply my conclusions based on the available evidence. Some of the references are examples from much larger bodies of research, but where there were larger, meta-analytic studies available, I tried to reference those to make it clear that I wasn't cherry-picking the data. The endnotes also include a few details and brief discussions that I thought were interesting but a bit tangential from the issue at hand, so if you're interested in diving more deeply into a specific issue here, it may be worth it to you to wade through the back of the book, where the reference material includes many links to articles and other online resources.

# Introduction:
# Therapy works, but
# fewer people are going

In December of 2013, I attended the Evolution of Psychotherapy conference not far from Disneyland. In this once-every-few-years gathering of therapists from around the world, many of leading clinicians and researchers in the United States present their findings to thousands of practitioners eager to learn at the foot of the masters.

One of those masters was Marsha Linehan. Years earlier, she developed a form of treatment for Borderline Personality Disorder called Dialectical Behavior Therapy. Linehan was at the conference not just to talk about her work, but to actually demonstrate specific components of it, using volunteers from the audience as stand-ins for patients.

Like the other therapists who came to see Linehan talk, I was particularly excited to see how she worked. All too often in therapy we read about others' theories, and try them out the way *we* think they should be done. But any opportunity to see the person who developed the model show how *that person* thinks it should be done is especially educational.

As the audience settled in and Linehan began her talk, the audio equipment in the room malfunctioned. Linehan had a big audience, and it was clear she wasn't normally a yeller. While hardly soft-spoken, even her efforts at being as loud as she could forced us in the crowd to lean in to hear. We did so willingly. Linehan is a fantastic storyteller, about both her model and her own journey in developing it.

And then, in the audience, there was a sound like a tiny train crash.

You are probably familiar with the sound. Someone not too far away reaches their hand into a foil bag for a snack, making that sharp, vaguely metallic crunch each time they touch the walls of the bag. All of us in the audience had paid hundreds of dollars to hear people like Linehan share their work, and now many of us couldn't hear her at all.

I was particularly fascinated by the reaction of the crowd around the woman making noise in the audience. Dozens of people – all of us therapists, remember – were noticing and reacting to the noise, but no one was saying anything to her about it. We were rolling our eyes. We were poking our neighbors. We were giving the woman an occasional dirty look. But nobody said a word, and these nonverbal messages didn't seem to be getting through. The woman kept on obliviously enjoying her snack.

I can't make this point strongly enough: This woman was surrounded by psychotherapists – *society's experts in behavior change* – and not one of us dared to directly address this woman's behavior, in spite of the fact that it was a relatively simple behavior that was having an immediate negative impact on us.

If this is the norm for our field, I thought, no wonder people aren't going to therapy! If those of us sitting around this woman are representative of the larger field, then an awful lot of us lack the nerve to actually tell clients what we think needs to change for the client to have a better life. That's *the very thing most people pay a therapist to tell them.* Making things worse was the realization that I was no better. I was fascinated at what was happening, but I wasn't confronting it.

Several minutes went by before another audience member, who had actually been a fair distance away when the noise started, said something to her. Her response was perfectly appropriate. She apologized, said she didn't realize she was bothering anyone, and quickly put the food away. I could see the instant relief on the faces of those around her, and the redirection of attention to the stage. Thinking about it another way, when a therapist pointed out the impact of what this woman was doing, she responded accordingly, and changed her behavior. I came away from the whole thing with no ill feeling toward the woman (we all sometimes do things that annoy others without knowing it), and a lot of curiosity about all of us therapists who had let our frustration build around her.

While I learned a lot from Linehan that morning, I left the conference feeling more than a little sheepish, and thinking more about our field. What does it say about us that the very thing we present ourselves as experts at doing, we struggle to do even among ourselves, even for a mild and easily resolvable problem?

This incident led me down the path of the book you are reading now. I began thinking about where we are as a profession, we therapists, from a larger social and economic point of view. I wondered for the first time about big-picture questions I had never considered in graduate school or up to that point in my career. Who are we as the collective professionals called therapists? Are we good at what we do, and what does that even mean? Are we meaningfully different from the therapists who came before us? And as I began searching for answers, I found a very troubling picture. The current state of the profession, it seems, can be summed up in a sentence:

Therapy works incredibly well, but fewer people are going.

# Therapy works

There is simply no scientific basis today to argue that psychotherapy is ineffective. Literally hundreds of studies involving thousands of therapists and tens of thousands of patients over several decades consistently demonstrate therapy's effectiveness for an overwhelming majority of those who engage in it.

There are several ways to measure this. Some researchers use a statistic called *effect size*, others use specific measures of client reports of behavior change, while still others use cost-effectiveness measures to assign monetary value to our work. Somewhat newer to the field is the use of brain imaging to measure the direct biological impact of therapy. In all cases, the evidence is clear: Therapy works.

Judging from effect size (a statistic that researchers use to measure the strength of one thing's impact on another), the impact of psychotherapy seems to be exponentially greater than the well-accepted practice of taking aspirin to reduce heart attacks.[1] It's much more effective than even the best obesity prevention programs for adolescents.[2] In addition to these and the other interventions shown in Table 1, psychotherapy has greater impact than the flu vaccine, cataract surgery, and a wide variety of other well-accepted medical interventions.[3]

Perhaps the strongest support for paying for psychotherapy (whether you're looking at this as an individual, or as an insurance company) comes from cost-effectiveness studies. Time after time, studies show that, on average, people who engage in psychotherapy reduce their overall health-care costs after the therapy more than enough to cover the cost of the therapy itself. Researchers call this an "offset effect," and it's been demonstrated for therapy overall as well as for several specific types of therapy.[4] When one particular form of therapy called Multisystemic Therapy was tested with families whose kids were encountering the juvenile justice system for the first time, it showed a return on investment of more than $5 in reduced long-term juvenile justice system costs for every $1 spent on therapy.[5] That kind of return on investment for any health care program (or, really, *any social program*) is virtually unheard of.

**Table 1. Typical effect sizes of selected health care interventions**

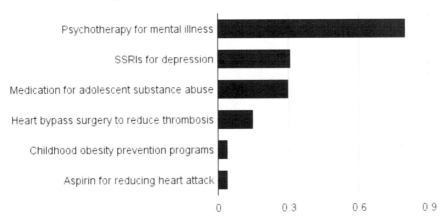

*Source data: Several.[6]*

Newest to the field is the use of neuroimaging processes to measure the impact of therapy. Not only can therapy improve functioning, there is significant evidence that therapy literally heals the brain. "Psychotherapists are applied neuroscientists," according to Louis Cozolino, whose book *The Neuroscience of Psychotherapy* lays out the research supporting this conclusion. The therapeutic relationship "establishes an emotional and biological context conducive to neural plasticity." Therapy focused on stress, anxiety, or depression can repair neurological deficits associated with these problems. This is perhaps most evident in studies of trauma, where therapy has been shown to have a profound effect on brain functioning.[7]

All of this data from all of these different angles offers a clear, singular truth: *Therapy works*. And yet, in spite of this clear and convincing evidence, fewer people are going.

# Increasing access, decreasing use

Changes in law and technology have made it easier than ever for a prospective client to access mental health care. New requirements for US residents to have health insurance (and for that insurance to cover mental health treatment), combined with new technologies for connecting with therapists remotely, mean that few people can legitimately claim that they couldn't access mental health care if they wanted it.

If you have health insurance, it probably covers psychotherapy. That hasn't always been the case. There has been a slow progression of mental health parity law at the federal level, with the most recent and comprehensive set of rules being issued in 2013.[8] Even these rules did not require health plans to cover mental health services.

*Parity* here simply means that *if* an insurance company is offering coverage for mental health issues, they have to provide that coverage on an even level with coverage for physical health issues. For companies that had been offering mental health coverage with higher deductibles or lower spending caps than what they applied to physical health, parity law offered them two choices: Improve their mental health coverage, or drop mental health coverage entirely. While many companies improved their coverage, there were some that simply discontinued covering mental health care at all. And of course, those who never covered mental health care in the first place still were not obligated to start.

While the new federal guidelines were helpful in improving insurance coverage for mental health care, many states already had their own parity laws. In some cases, these state laws came decades before the federal rules. Like the federal parity requirements, state laws typically required mental health coverage to be on par with physical health coverage *if it was offered at all*, which it didn't have to be.

The Affordable Care Act (you might know it as Obamacare, a term used with warmth by some and anger by others) went beyond parity. It required all health insurers selling coverage through federal and state-run insurance marketplaces to provide coverage for mental health and substance use disorders. With this requirement, the Affordable Care Act has provided new mental health coverage to millions of people who previously would have needed to pay out-of-pocket for therapy.

As these changes in law have provided US residents with greater access to mental health care, technology has been expanding its reach in ways that also have improved access. Telemedicine – that is, providing health care services through the use of technology – has been around since the early days of the telephone, but has only recently boomed in mental health care. Secure videoconferencing platforms can now make it feel like you're in the same room as a therapist hundreds of miles away. Some therapists will even work via text message or email if a videoconference connection isn't readily available.[9]

*Table 2. Percentage of US adults using mental health services in the past year*

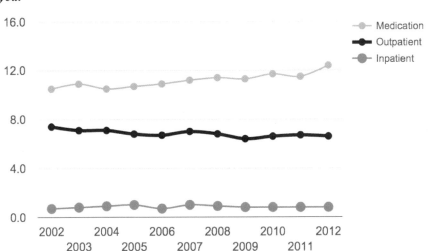

*Source data: Substance Abuse and Mental Health Services Administration.*

Together, these changes mean that almost everyone in the US could access the services of a therapist if they felt they needed one. While it is too soon to assess the full impact of the Affordable Care Act, even these massive increases in the availability of mental health care have so far seemingly had little impact on public utilization of therapy.

Studies continue to show a gradual long-term trend away from psychotherapy and toward prescription medication. Take, for instance, the 2013 study from the Substance Abuse and Mental Health Services Administration summarized in Table 2.[10] As you can see, the use of any outpatient care for mental health services decreased from 7.4 percent of the US adult population in 2002 to 6.6 percent in 2012. While the US adult population increased in that time, these figures still likely represent, at best, a flat line in the raw number of adults receiving outpatient mental health care in any given year.

*Table 3. Total annual US expenditure for psychotherapy, adjusted for inflation (in billions of 2007 dollars)*

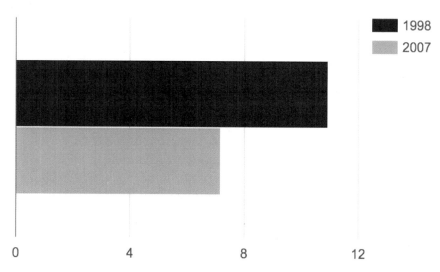

*Source data: Olfsun & Marcus, 2010.*[11]

Looking more specifically at psychotherapy (outpatient care in the table above includes psychotherapy, but includes other outpatient services as well), a separate study found that the percentage of the US population attending more than one therapy session in the year fell slightly between 1998 and 2007, to just over 3%. Those people who did go to therapy came for fewer sessions in 2007, on average (down by more than 15%, to just under eight) and paid less for it ($95 for an average session versus $123, a 23% decline). As you can see in Table 3, in total, Americans spent about *$3.7 billion less* on psychotherapy in 2007 than we had in 1998, after adjusting the 1998 numbers for inflation – a drop of more than a third.[12]

A quick aside on these numbers: Obviously, the 2007 numbers are a bit dated at this point. But they remain informative for a couple of reasons. First, their start point shows that the downward trend in the use of psychotherapy is not, by any reasonable definition, new. Psychotherapy's use in the US has been declining for quite some time. Second, the end point of this data comes *before* the economic downturn that led states and individual consumers alike to cut spending on mental health care even further. So it can't be argued that these numbers are simply the result of broader economic trends. Even when the overall economy was good, use of psychotherapy was declining.

# Decreasing use leads to decreasing pay

One of the predictable impacts of a decline in utilization of therapy is that it is getting harder for therapists to make a sustainable living. Over the past eight years of available data, salaries in the psychotherapy professions have not, on average, kept up with inflation (see Table 4 below).

This trend has been especially hard on psychologists, and arguably has been even worse than even the above data suggests. Looking at an earlier time frame of data, the American Psychological Association (APA) examined salaries for psychologists in a variety of different work settings. They found that from 2001 to 2009, psychologists who were direct service providers saw their salaries decrease by about 20% in inflation-adjusted dollars (see Table 5, next page). Based on the government data in Table 4, it seems likely that trend has only continued since.

*Table 4. Mean annual salaries in the psychotherapy professions, adjusted for inflation (in 2014 dollars)*

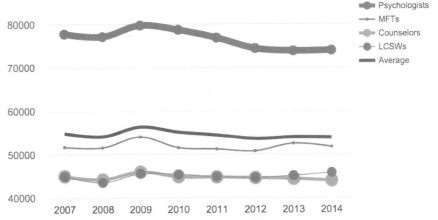

*Source data: US Bureau of Labor Statistics.*[13] *It's worth a trip to the endnotes to understand the strengths and weaknesses of this data.*

*Table 5. Median salaries of APA members in selected positions, adjusted for inflation (in 2009 dollars)*

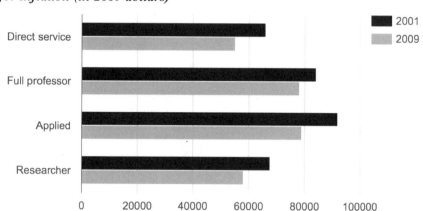

Source data: American Psychological Association Center for Workforce Studies.[14] "Applied" includes consulting, equipment design, personnel selection, and related non-clinical positions.

The combination of increasing training time and expense (an issue we'll examine in some detail in Task 2), salaries that are slowly losing purchasing power, and declining public spending on therapy raise meaningful questions about the long-term sustainability of the psychotherapy professions in their current form. If anything, therapists' salaries are so far surprisingly resilient, considering the decreases in what Americans are actually spending on therapy.

This combination of data also presents a contradiction. Considering how incredibly effective psychotherapy is, and the expansions in access to care offered by technology and changes in public policy, why are *fewer* people going? Why are those in emotional distress choosing other treatment options instead?

## The client experience

The National Alliance on Mental Illness (NAMI) teamed with Harris Interactive for a 2009 report on the experiences of people with depression.[15] Harris surveyed more than 500 people living with depression to learn more about the care they received, and how they felt about it. Much of what Harris and NAMI found was not surprising (for example, more than half reported that their primary care physician was their primary treatment provider for depression, and two-thirds noted that medication was their primary form of treatment). Some of it, however, was telling: More than 80% of those who had been in therapy reported that *they* had discontinued treatment; of those, more than a quarter said they had done so because of cost.

Two-thirds reported that medication was their current primary treatment. Only 16% reported that counseling was their primary treatment, which equals the combined total of those using prayer, exercise, herbal remedies, yoga, and animal therapy. But this stopped me in my tracks: Those who had used exercise, prayer, and animal therapy were more likely to find their chosen methods "extremely" or "quite a bit" helpful (40, 47, and 54%, respectively), than those who had used counseling (36%; see Table 6).

Given how much data there is to support the effectiveness of therapy, why would so many more people find other methods more helpful? And why did nearly two-thirds of those who had used therapy *not* find it very helpful?

*Table 6. Percentage of users finding various depression treatments "extremely" or "quite a bit" helpful*

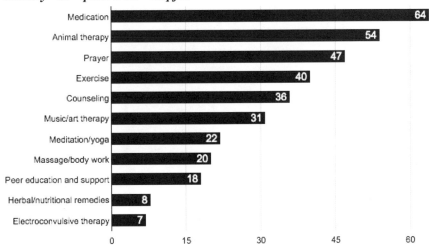

*Source data: NAMI/Harris Interactive.*[16]

A careful reading of the data showed that many people struggling with depression had at least *tried* therapy. It also showed that many of these same people had stopped therapy for reasons different from it not having the potential to work: It was too expensive (27%), I wanted to see if I could make it on my own (20%), I didn't like my provider (19%), and I couldn't find a good provider (14%) were all common responses. None of these are problems caused by the easy availability of medication, a common scapegoat we therapists use when trying to explain why our profession is falling out of favor. These factors instead represent failings on our end. We can't easily blame others for the fact that fully a third of those who discontinued therapy did so because they couldn't find a provider they thought was good or likeable.

The NAMI study is just one analysis, but it provides a useful perspective on the problems that face the psychotherapy field. When patients think that therapy is pretty good, but that other options work better, it could be said that we have a *competition* problem – that we need to demonstrate that our way is preferable to other ways. We can do this by focusing on how therapy gets to the root of the problem and creates long-term change, where other methods are temporary patches. As one example, a recent study showed therapy having a much more lasting effect on insomnia than the clearly more convenient and less expensive, but also less permanent, solution of taking sleeping pills.[17]

When patients think that therapy isn't very useful to them *regardless* of what other methods are available, it could be said that we have a *reputation* problem. We need to better explain what we do and why it works, and we need to make sure practitioners are accessible who are seen as being effective and trustworthy. We also need to do a better job of either retraining or removing those therapists who don't do their jobs very well, for the benefit of the field as a whole. As I mentioned at the beginning here, therapy in general is tremendously effective. However, there do appear to be meaningful differences in the effectiveness of individual therapists, even when working with similar populations. We'll discuss that issue in more detail later in this book.

The NAMI data showed that we currently appear to have *both* problems: therapy isn't seen as competing well against other services, and our reputation as a profession is not as strong as it could be. Notice, though, that the solutions to both do not rely on other groups – they call for tasks that we as professionals need to accomplish. You'll see this as a running theme through this book, one that leaves me very optimistic about the kinds of changes that can occur in the near future. We can solve both of these problems. We don't have to wait for others to do it for us.

# Avoiding the scapegoats

There is a natural tendency, when talking about these kinds of major shifts in the psychotherapy field, to seek out scapegoats. The nation's pharmaceutical companies, known together as Big Pharma, is commonly called out. So is government. Physicians are blamed for handing out medication when they should be referring for therapy. Social stigma is often held up as a concern, though its cause often isn't made any more specific than "society." Even movies and television are held up as reasons why the public doesn't seek out therapy, as they often depict therapists as unethical or incompetent.

The nice thing about scapegoats, of course, is that they absolve us from needing to take any action. They allow us to complain without any responsibility for change. It's as true here as it is when athletes blame the referee for their losing a game, or when political candidates blame anonymous donors for their losing an election. It's not that these outside forces have no impact, and indeed they can warrant useful attention. But by assigning them primary responsibility for the outcome, we retreat to a position of helplessness and are left to simply hope for better luck next time. What the athlete should be doing instead is practicing, so that a few bad calls become irrelevant to the outcome of the game. The candidate should focus on honing their message and building a bigger base of support for the next election.

The same principle applies to therapy. Big Pharma, government, physicians, and media all do have some influence. I'll mount an admittedly weak defense of each here, if only to make clear that their influence is often overstated. But the broader point is: *This isn't about them. It's about us.* We are not helpless, and we will not start to make the changes we need to make to earn public trust unless we first turn a mirror on ourselves.

### Big Pharma

We are, by any reasonable measure, a very highly medicated country. So many Americans now take psychotropic medication that traces of these medications show up in the drinking water of major cities.[18]

One reason for the high usage of prescription medication is that the US is one of only two industrialized countries that allow direct-to-consumer advertising of prescription medication.[19] The advertising campaigns of major drug companies do seem to be contributing to the idea that one need not be inconvenienced by psychotherapy or other health care treatments, that pills can now resolve many medical and mental health problems instead. In placebo-controlled medication trials, the effectiveness of placebos – *sugar pills, with no drug at all*, but made to look like drugs – has been rising dramatically.[20]

It is true, of course, that the major drug companies are large, international, for-profit enterprises. What they promise individuals with mental health problems is tempting: A moment a day to take a pill at home is far easier than trudging to the therapist's office to spend an hour a week there, and then spending much of the rest of the week trying to implement what was learned in therapy.

But it's also true that psychotropic drugs are quite effective for many of those who take them. For example, in that NAMI/Harris depression study, the intervention most likely to be seen as extremely or quite a bit helpful was medication (Table 6).

We don't do well to trot out the moral high horse when talking about drug companies or their products. They offer many the possibility of a faster and easier road to good health than what therapy can offer. The appeal of that possibility is obvious. Rather than judging drug companies and those who use their products, we have to see them as both competitors and collaborators in the mental health marketplace. We'll never convince clients to turn away from medication with a general "drugs are bad" stance, or by turning up our noses at an efficient form of treatment. We have to do the real work of competition, which means understanding brain science and being able to make the case for why therapy has the potential to be a more cost-effective and longer-lasting solution for many patients.

Lamenting therapists' struggle against the social influence of drug ads, researchers have noted that therapists don't have a "Big psychotherapy" to fight the influence of Big Pharma.[21] That led others to encourage the creation of such a thing.[22] It's an interesting but wholly unrealistic idea. Pharmaceutical companies spend about $5 billion a year *just on marketing* in the US,[23] easily dwarfing the entire annual budgets of the American Psychological Association, American Counseling Association, National Alliance of Social Workers, and American Association for Marriage and Family Therapy *combined*.

But consumer attitudes toward drug advertising already appear to be growing more skeptical.[24] They appear to increasingly understand the limitations of medication alone in offering lasting fixes, and seem to be increasingly distrustful of drug company claims. In fact, consumers routinely express a strong preference for psychotherapy over medication.[25] We have an opportunity to make the case for why consumers should return to us as trusted authorities in mental health care.

## Government

While the economic downturn of a few years ago is now at least tentatively in our rearview mirror, it led state governments around the country to slash more than $1.6 billion in general funds from public mental health care.[26] Fewer people in need were able to obtain services, and many therapists found themselves scrambling for work. While the federal government's moves to increase access to care through parity rules and Obamacare are worthy of praise, they seem to have had little practical impact in the utilization of outpatient therapy, at least based on the limited data available so far.

As the economy has recovered, many states have sought to restore some of the funding for mental health services that had been cut when the economy was weak. Interestingly, while the cuts often targeted psychotherapy, the restored money often did not. Wisconsin serves as a useful example here: A package of bills signed into law in 2014 restored about $4 million in state funding for mental health. But *none* of that money went to psychotherapy. Instead, it went toward crisis intervention, law enforcement, medical treatment, a jobs program, and peer supports.[27]

Government funding for research in mental health care also largely ignores therapy. Only about 5% of National Institute of Mental Health research funding goes toward clinical trials in psychotherapy,[28] and NIMH announced in 2014 that going forward it will focus almost exclusively on understanding the biology of mental illness.[29]

It would be neither fair nor accurate to accuse most government officials of indifference to mental health issues. In many cases, officials are tasked with making difficult choices about how to use limited funding for a long list of health care services that are each critical in their own way. However, to the degree that policymakers could be providing better support for mental health care and are choosing not to, a fair amount of the blame for this falls on us.

Research in family policy has shown that policymakers have a great hunger for clear, unbiased information on policies that impact families (including, presumably, health care issues), and all too often that hunger is not being met.[30] Elected officials often simply don't know who they can turn to in order to inform them on key policy decisions. We can support our professional organizations and count on them to do this type of outreach, but there are not nearly enough therapists involved in this effort. California has more than 100 state legislators and hundreds of others in key positions in state and county agencies. Professional associations can often afford little more than a single staffer and lobbyist to remain in contact with all of these officials, and they can't possibly keep up. We need more therapists directly involved in this work.

## Physicians

When faced with a mental health problem, most people don't immediately seek treatment from a therapist. They start by going to their physician.[31] This is, as you might expect, particularly true when some of their symptoms are physical (like fatigue, cramping, or insomnia). While doctors typically have had some training in mental health issues, many therapists lament that physicians don't refer to therapy more.

All too often I hear therapists wondering why more physicians don't automatically refer patients for therapy any time they prescribe psychotropic medication. Studies show that medication often works best when combined with therapy.[32] So why wouldn't this warrant an automatic referral? Again, though, this is an inappropriate transfer of responsibility away from us and onto outside, largely uncontrollable factors. Yes, medication often works best when combined with therapy – which *also means the reverse is true.* And yet most therapists certainly don't make automatic referrals for medication assessment.

It is arguable that neither referral direction should be automatic, and we will spend more time on the problem of medicalizing mental health care in Task 3 (Embrace science). We certainly could (and should) do a more effective job of working with physicians to ensure they understand when such referrals are warranted. But we also need to acknowledge that physicians are often simply responding to what patients say they want and need. Physicians' reluctance to refer clients to therapy could simply reflect patients' preference for quick fixes, specific requests for prescription drugs, or statements of unwillingness to attend therapy.

## Social stigma

There is still a stigma involved in seeking mental health care for many, particularly those from historically marginalized or oppressed groups. However, stigma is not as powerful a force in general as some would believe. In a 1997 survey of more than 1,000 participants, researchers (working on behalf of the APA) asked about factors that might keep the survey participant from seeking mental health treatment even when they thought it might be appropriate. The two choices that suggested stigma – concerns about others finding out, and concerns about what others would think of you – were the least popular answers, with fewer than a third saying they would be even somewhat important. In contrast, concerns about cost and insurance coverage topped the list, with 84% of respondents saying each of these would be somewhat or very important. More than three-fourths cited lack of confidence in the outcome of therapy as a somewhat or very important consideration.[33] This is not the only study to challenge the idea of stigma as a powerful force in the general population. A study of college undergraduates found strong disagreement with the idea that going to therapy is a sign of weakness.[34]

Stigma remains a powerful force for some, and indeed, it is a force worth actively fighting. This is especially true in minority communities. But most people aren't worried about what others will think of them if they seek therapy. They worry about whether it will work.

## Movies and television

Several studies have concluded that movies and television shows in the US tend to show therapists as incompetent, unethical, and even dangerous in their work.[35] In the first season of the television show *American Horror Story,* a therapist character described his practice like this:

"It's a great racket, too. Week after week, month after month, year after year, we collect checks, but deep down we know it doesn't work."

In a technical sense, I believe this character was also *undead*, so it's worth taking his statements with a bit of a grain of salt (or garlic – I get my horror creatures confused). As therapists, we can do that. For the public, it may not be so easy.

Seeing portrayals like this steers people away from therapy by influencing their expectations of the process. Those who have been to therapy before appear more likely to be able to understand these portrayals as fiction, but for those who have never seen a therapist, movies and TV are often all they know about what therapy looks like. If they get the impression that typical therapy involves meeting for an hour a week with someone who doesn't care about them or who is likely to disregard professional standards, of course they're less likely to call on a therapist in a time of need.[36]

While the use of psychotherapy is declining, it is certainly still common enough that therapy will continue to frequently appear in television, movies, and other media. It is unfortunate, then, that many of the therapists who decry media portrayals of therapy are the same ones who avoid the media as if it carries disease. While therapists naturally need to use caution in making public statements, media portrayals of therapy don't get better by therapists avoiding microphones. They get better when ethical, responsible professionals make their faces and their voices known. This can balance media portrayals of incompetent or unethical therapists with images of knowledgeable, caring, responsible professionals.

::

The problems we face as modern psychotherapists are not, by and large, the result of these outside groups chipping away at our work. These outside forces do have some influence, but we are in little position to criticize until we have our own proverbial house in order. Our competition and reputation problems are in large part the fruits of our own complacency. Because we have a field that is so tremendously effective, it can be hard to muster the energy or courage to change. But we do have it in us, and it's needed now.

## The risk we face

Admittedly, the very title of this book begs the question: Saving psychotherapy *from what*? The field isn't going to *die* in the foreseeable future, at least not in the absolute sense. There are simply too many good therapists actively engaged in their work for that to happen. There are also too many professional organizations fighting the good fight to keep their members happy while improving public access to care.

No, what I worry about is the family of psychotherapy professions fading into a shadow of what they could and should be. I see two distinct possibilities for how our field will look 30 years from now.

If we stay the course we're on, psychotherapy will become a field *of the wealthy, by the wealthy, and for the wealthy*. The professionals will be largely made up of those wealthy enough to afford the extensive training, as requirements continue to climb and the cost of education stays on its runaway course. Therapy clients will be split in two groups, like plastic surgery clients: One group of those who are wealthy enough to afford the indulgence, and one group of the most seriously disfigured.

Therapists will groan about encroachments on their "turf" by applied behavioral analysts, life coaches, and even untrained peer counselors, and policymakers will respond by pointing out that these other professionals are necessary because there simply aren't enough trained therapists to meet the public need. Therapists will continue to claim the mantle of science when it is convenient to us, such as when we want to use outcome data to open new job opportunities, but on an individual level we will continue to actively *avoid* changing our practices to fit with science or subjecting our own work to any kind of meaningful accountability.

The public will generally see us as something of a hybrid of plastic surgeons for the mind and palm readers. The field will not die, but it will struggle to find a foothold for continued respectability.

At the other end of the spectrum is the future I believe is both possible and deserved. A future is possible where the public trusts therapists because the primary barrier to entry into the profession is skill, not wealth. Where our training processes require us to prove ourselves in a number of meaningful ways, but as long as we are able to do so, we actually have *less* training than is required today, as the field has moved toward training only in those areas proven to be strongly linked with safe and effective practice. While there remains a spectrum of therapists in terms of those who practice "by the book" and those who see their craft as more of an art form, we all embrace accountability to our clients and can demonstrate that what we do – both collectively and on an individual level – works. We see science not as a threat to therapy but as one of its biggest supports, as neuroimaging continues to demonstrate the healing power of all forms of psychotherapy on the brain. And when a prospective client asks what kind of therapist you are, that question means something, because we have improved our ability to define and discuss just what it is we do.

That future, the one I hope for, may seem at first like a pipe dream. And to be sure, our choice is not either/or. While the two futures described above represent opposite ends of a spectrum, we also could land somewhere in between. But if nothing else, I hope you gather from these pages that I am *relentlessly* optimistic about the work we do and what our future could hold. There is nothing in that ideal future I have described that we would have to rely on others for, or that we must sit back and hope goes our way. *Every part* of that better future is up to us.

I know we can get there. In the remaining chapters of this book, I'll describe how we can do it – and how you are an essential part of that change.

## The five tasks

The remainder of this text is focused not just on convincing you that therapists *can* save psychotherapy, but on detailing *how* that can be accomplished. There is no single magic bullet that can save our field. But there are a number of actions that we can take both individually and collectively that will ensure the field of psychotherapy not only survives to the next century, but expands and thrives, effectively serving *all* segments of the public, not just the rich and the desperate.

Getting to this future, as I see it, breaks down into five tasks. First, we need to **clarify our purpose and values.** While the psychotherapy profession has formally existed for more than 100 years (and certainly, community healers using precursors to talk therapy predate the formal profession by thousands of years), we are surprisingly vague when it comes to describing ourselves and our purpose. This causes problems for anyone on the outside looking in. If your friend was having an affair, and suffering a great deal of emotional pain over it, would you send him to see a therapist? Working with such a client, some therapists would encourage the breakup of the marriage, while others would fight to keep the marriage together. Still others would aim to be a therapeutic Switzerland, neutral in all matters, and likely leaving the client wondering whether the therapist has anything that could actually qualify as expertise.

Individual therapists have morals and values, but training in therapy teaches new therapists to keep their own values out of the room, so as to avoid imposing them on clients. The psychotherapy profession also has values, and these are the ones that new therapists are told to adopt. But in many cases these values offer little meaningful guidance to a therapist struggling to determine how best to help a client in need. To an outsider, and even to ourselves, it is not always clear which values and which constituents we truly serve. Once you understand this, it may be much easier to forgive clients – and physicians – their distrust of us.

The second task is to **fix the process of therapist training and licensure.** It is simply unconscionable that we require such expensive education and training for jobs that may not pay enough over a lifetime to make this a sound investment. Interestingly, the American Psychological Association seems to be understanding this and taking action on it – yet the requirements for the master's-level professions of clinical social work, professional counseling, and marriage and family therapy are seeing their training requirements get *stricter*. Most alarming in the discussion of therapist training is how largely uninformed by science the current requirements are.

The best current research suggests that clinical skills typically plateau after about 150 hours of clinical experience. Yet for most psychotherapy professions in most states, roughly *3,000* supervised hours of experience must be documented before one qualifies to even be tested for licensure. Repairing the therapist training process can absolutely be done in a way that benefits the public without compromising client safety, and this section will detail how.

The third task is to **embrace science.** The field of neurobiology has come a long way in the past 20 years, and advances in brain imaging technology are tremendously supportive of psychotherapy as a process that doesn't just make patients feel better – it actually *heals the brain*. Yet many therapists ignore, belittle, or actively disregard this science. As a result, tremendous potential for advances in the treatment of mental illness are being made not by psychotherapists but by drug manufacturers, biologists, and others who have little to no interest in supporting psychotherapy. Too many therapists take an either-or approach to hard science that results in their discounting the very idea of knowledge – undercutting the idea that a therapist could be an expert in anything. I know of few better examples of cutting off one's nose to spite their face.

The fourth task is to **accept accountability**. More than once I have heard the quote (attributed to different sources) that psychotherapy is the only health profession where you can practice the same way you did 30 years ago and *not* be considered hopelessly out of date. That needs to change. We must accept that entry into the profession should be contingent on demonstrating clinical effectiveness, that some therapies should not continue to be practiced (and, indeed, that we must also do a better job at re-educating or removing those *therapists* who violate professional standards), and that our acceptance of the uniqueness of each clinical case is not carte blanche for any therapist to apply any treatment they want, at any time, without so much as checking in with the science to see whether their chosen approach has *ever* demonstrated effectiveness with their client's particular problem. While therapeutic models differ little in their effectiveness, there do appear to be meaningful differences in the effectiveness of *therapists*. This is a hard truth, and one that must be acted upon. Accountability will not stifle innovation in psychotherapy service delivery; it instead will allow us a newfound freedom to creatively conceptualize and deliver therapy.

Underlying each of these tasks is the most important of them all: **Take it personally.** When we speak of decreased utilization of therapy, and public distrust in therapists, we're not talking in the abstract about other therapists in other cities getting fewer calls. It means that *your* prospective clients, in *your* town, don't trust *you.* When we talk about the difficulty therapists have making a living, we're talking about the possibility that *your* practice will not be sustainable.

# Taking it personally

My fiancée tells the story of the best sermon she ever heard as a girl growing up in the Catholic Church. The priest began by telling the congregation that he often heard the same lament from those who sought his counsel: they weren't sure how to protect their families and direct their energies in times that the world seemed to be in upheaval. They asked him questions like "How can I give to charity when I'm so worried my own family will wind up with nothing?" and "How can I make sure my children stay on the right path?" Roughly translated, the priest said, these questions all amounted to "How can I keep everything from falling apart?"

The world is a troubled and trying place, he explained, and the church offered eternal answers more clearly than it offered immediate ones.

But having spent much time wrestling with these questions from parishioners in thought and prayer, the priest said, he had learned to offer a simple response.

*Gather your family for dinner. Talk with them, Eat with them. Let them know they have a safe place to return to in your home. If you set out to save the world, you will surely fail. But if you set out to teach your children love and compassion, every time another family is in your home, they will also see this love and compassion, and may be encouraged to try it themselves. Fifty families behaving in this way soon becomes a hundred, then a thousand. And then, by your hand, the world is saved.*

He wasn't talking about spreading a religious message; he even expressly discouraged it. He was talking about taking *personal* responsibility for *community* well-being. It is far too easy to see a large problem and assume it requires a large solution, when often a group of people engaging in small, individual solutions can be every bit as effective, even more.

This is especially relevant to the larger trends outlined here. Fewer people are coming to outpatient psychotherapy. Our standing in the public eye and among other health care fields is at best a flat line; at worst, it is actively eroding. These changes did not happen all at once, through a single television ad for medication, or through a single government budget cut. Our professional standing improves or erodes one person at a time.

When you provide effective therapy to a client, that person or family comes away impressed not just with you, but impressed with the thing you provide: psychotherapy. Some clients may have the knowledge and experience to further narrow this positive association, and to sing the praises of the specific type of therapy you performed. But many don't know or care about what particular theoretical model you used. They just care that they found a therapist they could trust, went to therapy, and it worked for them. That's what they will tell their friends and co-workers. And through a single client, you have improved the standing of your own work *as well as the standing of the profession*, at least in the eyes of all those who hear from your client about their experience.

Of course, the reverse can also be true. A therapist who is perpetually late, who puts little effort into their work with clients, who isn't successful in their work – or, worse, who behaves unethically – doesn't just harm their own reputation by doing so. Their clients will similarly associate their experience with therapy in general, not just the one therapist in particular. This is one of the strongest arguments for confronting and (where it's legally allowed) reporting the unethical behavior of your professional colleagues. Their behavior doesn't just hurt that client and it doesn't just hurt that therapist. It hurts *you*, and me, and every other therapist who now has to push against the notion that therapists in general behave in unprofessional or even unethical ways. That belief is held by a surprisingly large number of people, and it will not change if we stand around waiting for other therapists to get better.

The only way the problems outlined in this book can be fixed is if each one of us takes on personal responsibility for the well-being of our professional community. This can be done in ways that not only will benefit the field, but will also directly benefit you and your practice – and are not terribly inconveniencing. In other words, these small steps can help us save the therapy professions as a group, but for most therapists, I think you'll also get your time and money's worth on an individual level.

::

There is some collective action necessary to solve these problems, to be sure, and much of that can be achieved through our professional associations *if* they have your active participation and support. I'll talk more later about the reasons why newer therapists are avoiding their professional associations, and why I think you should join anyway. But thinking about these professional challenges as big-picture struggles creates a diffusion of responsibility, where we largely keep to ourselves except to occasionally ask for updates on how the battle is going. The problems here impact each one of us individually, and they call for changes in *individual* practice, not just policy. At the end of each of the four chapters that follow, I will outline how you can start *right now* to build a therapy practice that is better for you, better for your clients, and salvation for your profession. Many of the specific steps I describe here are actually relatively easy, and I think you will be surprised at just how much they can improve both the effectiveness of your work and your enjoyment of it.

As you can see, this book is not simply about averting the future we currently seem to be headed toward. It is about making a better future for psychotherapy and those who practice it possible. A future is possible where it does not take hundreds of thousands of dollars to become a therapist, where physicians and the public know and respect the work psychotherapists do both individually and as a group, where our professional titles have meaning. This kind of future benefits therapists, sure, but it also will benefit the larger communities where we live, by making the services of therapists more available, more reliable, more transparent, and more accountable.

Getting there does not depend centrally on the actions of lawyers, lobbyists, researchers, or professional associations, though all of those are certainly important. It depends on the actions that *individual practicing therapists, interns, and students* can take right now to create a brighter professional future for all of us.

If you are a therapist, the remaining chapters of this book are a call to action. It applies at every career level, from student to seasoned licensee. It is not for your colleagues, your teachers, or your future self.

It is for you. Starting today.

# Task 1:
# Clarify our purpose and values

*You have been the therapist to Janelle and her husband Ray for four sessions of couple therapy. Their marriage is highly strained, and they have two young children. Ray had abused alcohol earlier in life, but soon after the birth of his second child – and faced with Janelle's threat of kicking him out of the home – he went into treatment. He has been sober for four years. One afternoon, he calls your office in tears. He had a relapse, binge drinking for several hours. He is worried that if Janelle finds out, she will follow through with her threat from four years ago, and kick him out of the house. He pleads with you to keep his secret, and asks where to go for help.*

*Lex and his long-time girlfriend Annalee have three children. Lex has been coming to individual therapy to address severe anxiety symptoms that he believes are linked with his dissatisfaction in the relationship with Annalee. They argue frequently, and while they have never been violent with one another, their shouts have resulted in police at their house several times. Lex calls late in the day on a Wednesday to cancel the next day's session, and to inform you that he will be moving out of state. He has a job and a place to stay lined up through a friend. The conflict with Annalee has gotten to be too much for him to bear, he says, and while he is pained with the prospect of leaving his children, he believes the move is the only way he will be able to find relief.*

These are the kinds of problems we psychotherapists face every day. While some clients come to us with a clear set of mental health symptoms as their only concern, more often we see clients whose emotional struggles exist in the larger context of full and challenging lives. We know our job is to reduce suffering where we can, but in cases like these, whose suffering takes precedence?

Let's consider Lex first. Whose needs should be prioritized? Lex's needs, since he is the client? The needs of the children, since they are vulnerable to negative impacts from their father's absence? The needs of Annalee, who may become the sole provider for three children – and who may not even know that Lex is planning to leave?

The psychotherapy professions offer no answer to this question. Some therapists will prioritize Lex as the client, acknowledging the pain of his choice but respecting his right to make it, and encouraging him to find relief and ultimately happiness in whatever way he can. Others will prioritize the children, even having never met them, out of a belief that the needs of children trump the needs of their parents in many instances, and that the greater good is served by improving the children's lives. And still others will prioritize Annalee, out of a broader commitment to justice that argues Lex does not have the right to simply dump responsibility for the children onto her.

Each of these reflects a value that we as psychotherapists lay claim to in our work. Prioritizing Lex goes along with a value of *autonomy*, respect for a client's right to self-determination. Prioritizing the children aligns with *beneficence*, the desire to maximize the positive impact of therapy. And prioritizing Annalee reflects a strong identification with *justice*. These, along with *fidelity* (upholding truth and loyalty) and *nonmalfeasance* (avoiding harm), are considered to be the core values of psychotherapists.[37] And together, they don't really tell us anything about what the therapist should do here.

Reading about Janelle and Ray, who relapsed with alcohol, you might have had some clearer reactions. Therapists who work with couples and families are encouraged to have policies about whether they will hold secrets for individuals within the family unit. There are good arguments to be made in multiple directions on this, but reading about Ray you may have thought, *Whatever my policy is, I'm sticking to it.* That goes with the value of fidelity. You might have also thought about the possibility that Ray was intoxicated at the time of the call, and so you wanted to keep him from driving. Your efforts to keep him (and others on the road) safe from harm reflect the value of non-malfeasance. But after that, where are you left?

The same questions arise with Ray and Janelle that arose with Lex about whose interests you are protecting, and why. If the field does not offer clear guidance about whose interests you are to uphold in cases like this, how do you begin to make that choice on your own? Perhaps more importantly, how can a prospective client know what to expect when they come to therapy for the first time? Will they be seeing a therapist who believes in clients pursuing individual happiness, or one who believes instead in commitment to work and family?

Therapists and the public share a problem with psychotherapy. *We don't know who or what it is that therapists are fighting for.* Psychologists and counselors primarily see individuals, but that's by no means a guarantee that the therapist will put the welfare of that individual above the welfare of others. And just because a therapist works with a whole family, that doesn't mean they will necessarily put the welfare of the family above the individual.

Instead, many of us kick the proverbial can to the client. We develop a treatment plan based on their goals and desires. As long as those goals seem reasonable enough, we do our best to help them get there. But how we get there, and what we prioritize along the way, remains a mystery to the client. For someone unfamiliar with therapy, the experience can be a bit like getting into a taxi wearing a blindfold: They tell the driver where they want to go, and can only trust that the driver knows how to get there and will drive in the right direction. They have no way of knowing whether the taxi is safe, or what the driver thinks is important (speed, safety, adventure, a scenic view, or possibly just collecting a huge fare). The driver offers no evidence that they've gotten anyone anywhere safely before, an issue we'll return to later in this book. They simply tell the passenger, "Trust me." Would you?

# The personal and the professional meet

Hopefully your choice of profession reflects, on at least some level, what your personal values are. You could have chosen a career in law or finance or engineering, after all, and perhaps made more money. Choosing to become a therapist suggests, if nothing else, that your desire to help those in need is stronger than your desire to be rich.

Strange, then, that from the time we therapists begin graduate school, much of our training focuses on minimizing or even disavowing our personal values. Don't get me wrong, I don't think that your personal beliefs should trump your professional responsibilities. Julea Ward and Jennifer Keeton sued their graduate programs after they were told they can't use their religious beliefs as an excuse to refuse treatment to gay and lesbian clients,[38] and I tend to side with the universities there. The non-discrimination clauses in each mental health profession's code of ethics are strong, and I think they should outweigh an individual's desire to discriminate. But in areas where our professional values are unclear or undefined, you have to be able to make decisions based on *something*. We do new therapists no favors by suggesting that their personal values become irrelevant the moment they walk into the therapy room.

Nowhere is this question of professional values more evident than in our field's struggle over whether to give advice. When I teach law and ethics to aspiring counselors and family therapists in a university setting, or discuss legal and ethical issues with therapists of all kinds in conferences and continuing education workshops, I am consistently surprised at how resistant many therapists are to the simple *concept* of giving advice in their professional roles. Simply telling a client what to do, I often hear, is insensitive at best, and unethical at worst. It disregards client autonomy and fosters dependence. It ignores their culture and values, substituting instead the "knowledge" of the therapist.

Based on the transitions in the field I've seen in my career, I'm not surprised to see such resistance to advice-giving. Modern training in psychotherapy places such an emphasis on the therapist as collaborator, and on honoring the unique circumstances of each individual case, that students in the psychotherapy professions are often frightened out of what I believe is the therapist's appropriate role. They're not just told that advice-giving should be limited, they get the implicit – or in some cases, plainly stated – message that giving advice makes them *bad therapists*.

Even discussing the issue of advice brings forth an important question: **What should the role of the professional therapist be?** Are we essentially paid friends for clients, walking with them through difficult moments in their life and offering emotional support, but steadfastly refusing to tell them what we think they should do? Are we fundamentally scientists, exercising the knowledge the field has developed to better the lives of our clients? While there is certainly room for differences among us on this question, based on personal beliefs, theoretical orientations, and so on, are there limitations to what we can be as therapists, or do we have carte blanche to take on whatever role we want?

To best examine this question, it is worth stepping back a bit. Rather than focusing first on the word "therapist," consider what it means to be a "professional." Not every job qualifies as a *profession*; the term suggests higher status. *Professions* include things like law, medicine, and accounting, among others. If I were to ask you what makes a certain field a profession rather than just a job or career, you might rightly point out things like:

- A professional code of ethics that all members of the profession agree to follow
- Advanced education and training
- Some kind of government license or certification
- A position of status in the community, by virtue of the other items listed here

All of those are accurate, and you may be able to list more as well. Ultimately, a profession is defined by an exchange with the larger community: A professional is entrusted to work in sensitive or specialized areas in exchange for doing the training, getting the license, and adhering to higher standards of behavior than would be expected for others. In other words, if you are willing to do the work to get there, and follow professional standards once you're there, you will be trusted and held up as society's experts in your particular professional area. Such status comes with benefits, but also responsibilities.

Consider, then, the exchange involved in becoming a professional therapist. The community around you entrusts you to work with those who are mentally and emotionally suffering. By virtue of your training, you have unique and specialized knowledge about mental health and behavior change that the overwhelming majority of people in the community do not have. (There are problems with therapist training, which we'll address in the next chapter, but those don't negate the truth of that sentence.) Among the benefits of becoming a therapist is being recognized as an emotional healer, someone who can and should receive pay just for sitting and talking with clients about their problems. Among the responsibilities, codified in each psychotherapy profession's code of ethics, is that you exercise your specialized knowledge to better the lives of your clients and to better the community around you.

I believe that this agreement we make with the communities we serve leads to a clear conclusion. *Therapists who refuse to give advice are failing to fulfill their responsibilities as professionals.*

Thankfully, we all do give advice, even if we claim not to. At the beginning of this section I talked about how resistant some students and even some experienced therapists can be to the concept of giving advice. They're typically not so resistant to the *actuality* of it.

We all give advice in therapy. We can't help it. Any question we ask, any statement we make, comes with an implicit instruction. If I tell a client, "Can you turn to your partner and say to them what you just said to me," I am giving advice. If you assign homework to your clients, you are giving advice – the whole idea of homework, after all, is that doing the thing you have assigned will advance the therapy and improve their lives.

Some therapists draw a meaningful distinction between small-scale advice, like assigning tasks in therapy, and large-scale advice, like pushing a client to stay in their job or their relationship when the client is considering leaving. Also codified in our codes of ethics is the idea that therapists do not make major life decisions for their clients – that we respect the autonomy of clients, their right to choose for themselves the path they wish to take.

To be clear, I am not advocating that you make such decisions for your clients. I'm also not entirely sure how you could. As a therapist, you will not be the one packing up the client's desk or clothes if they make the decision to leave their work or their home. They'll be doing that. And you're probably not going to be the one announcing the client's departure. They'll be doing that. As long as your clients are relatively well-functioning people, you can (and, I will argue, should) *influence* their decision, but you can't *make it for them.*

If we choose to offer our thoughts about which path might be better for the clients, based on our knowledge of them, our clinical experience, and our understanding of the long-term impacts of such decisions based on current science, and if we appropriately describe the limitations inherent in each of these, is it so unreasonable to think that clients can put our guidance into the proper context? (Again, I'm assuming that the clients involved are relatively well-functioning adults; it is appropriate to be more cautious about this with children or others where offering too much direction may foster dependency.) They'll consider it alongside the advice they receive from friends, family members, and others they trust. Ultimately, they'll make the best decision they can, based on the information available to them.

The idea that advising a client of our professional opinion on a major life decision is equivalent to *making the decision for the client* is insulting to the client. It's infantilizing. It demonstrates an assumption that the client either does not have or would not use any of their own capable judgment. It rejects their ability to take our perspective under consideration as one of many. And ultimately, the belief that *advising* equals *imposing* leads therapists to try as hard as they can to avoid saying anything at all that might be heard as a recommendation. That can be tremendously frustrating to clients. Their frustration is understandable.

Consider again the exchange we make with the larger community when we become professional therapists. We have specialized training that most people in the community don't have. We have clinical experience working repeatedly with struggles that many people experience only once or twice in a lifetime. And we have a scientific knowledge base that, while not necessarily predictive on an individual level, at least offers some information on how these major life decisions *generally* turn out. In exchange for being held up as society's experts on mental health and behavior change, the community expects us to *use* that training, experience, and knowledge. Refusing to inform clients of how we see various possible decisions panning out for them is refusing to hold up our end of the bargain.

Put another way, what do you think it is your clients are paying you for?

The advice you give will necessarily reflect both your knowledge and a set of values. Those therapists who say they only advise in the context of the client's own values are not to be trusted; I have a hard time believing they would help a client who wants to become a better burglar, one who wants to more effortlessly cheat on their spouse, or one who wants to reduce the guilt they feel over molesting children. We all draw lines in the sand, and that's healthy. Our profession could eat us alive otherwise. It is generally, if not universally, accepted that therapy cannot be a value-free enterprise.[39] Rather than disavowing the existence or importance of our personal values, we would do better to acknowledge them for what they are, allow them to assist us when professional values offer no guidance,[40] and do these things consciously and transparently.

# Different professions, different values

Today's students in the mental health professions don't need to be trailblazers. They benefit from clear paths cut for them, in the forms of well-established training programs, clear standards of licensure, and professional associations that socialize them into their fields. While every new therapist has to figure out for themselves how they wish to specialize (if they want to at all), where they would like to work, and what models of therapy fit them best, we are past the stage of *forming* these fields and well into the stage of *curating* them.

There are benefits and drawbacks to this. On the plus side, once you decide that you would like to become a therapist, there are multiple, well-plowed paths to get there. Sure, there are meaningful barriers along all of those paths – primarily financial – but there's typically no need to battle someone else to make sure your profession exists.[41] You can know what dues will need to be paid to enter into your chosen field, and rest relatively well assured that if you are able to pay them, you can earn a professional license and the title that comes with it.

The main drawback of having such well-established paths to professional standing is that this naturally removes us from having to individually answer what are, at the early stages of development for any field, some key philosophical questions: *Why does this field need to exist? What makes it unique?* In fact, the psychotherapy professions have become so homogenized (especially at the master's degree level) that some students choose their course of study – and in so doing, their eventual profession – without any meaningful consideration at all of how a social worker, a counselor, and a family therapist differ from each other or from a psychologist. Rather, they choose the path that will lead them to licensure and employment the fastest.

I mean no judgment in saying this. It is actually a quite rational choice if you know that you want to help people by becoming a therapist, and you know that you have a limited supply of time, energy, and money. It also illustrates a stark reality: The master's-level professions have become so indistinguishable from one another that students don't really need to make sure that they are picking the best one for them. In the eyes of some students and much of the public, all forms of psychotherapists are pretty much the same.[42]

This reality can be especially troubling for psychologists, who – unlike the master's-level professions – have to complete a doctoral degree to achieve licensure. In spite of a graduate education that can be twice as long as a master's degree, and correspondingly much more expensive, many prospective clients and even some employers can view psychologists as just one kind of therapist among several.

The professions themselves don't do much to make this easier. In 2014, the ACA designed an infographic of "12 things you should know about professional counselors."[43] Only someone within the professions, steeped in their specific usage of language, would recognize thing #3, "Focus on wellness, career development, and client empowerment – a proactive approach to mental health," as being unique to counselors. To the public, that sounds pretty much like what all therapists do, with the possible exception of the career development piece. In fact, there *isn't a single thing among those 12* that is truly and wholly unique to counselors. Change the language just a bit on that third thing, and on thing #1's mention of educational degrees (counselors get degrees in counseling, as you would expect), and the infographic could just as easily and accurately be used by any psychotherapist.

It matters a great deal that clients, employers, and sometimes even therapists don't recognize the differences between different types of therapists. Without meaningful distinctions between professional groups, neither clients nor employers can easily make informed decisions about the kinds of professional services they are seeking, nor can they have reasoned expectations about what kind of services to expect. The end result is downward pressure on wages for all therapists since we are seen as interchangeable, and confusion or even concern among the public that we are somehow misrepresenting who we are.

With the possible exception of social work, the mental health professions today do little to distinguish their professional values from those of other mental health workers. There are good reasons for this, but the end result is confusion.

## History

This homogenizing of therapy professions, particularly at the master's level, is largely an artifact of how the professions evolved, with an emphasis on how they responded to the need for state licensure. The formations of the fields, though, occurred in response to very different societal needs – needs that can and should still guide the work of practitioners in the fields today, and that make a very useful place to begin a discussion of what the fields should value. Don't worry – an arduous history lesson isn't necessary or especially helpful here, so I'll keep this short and focused.

Of the psychotherapy professions, psychology's history is certainly the best known, with Freud and Jung being household names for much of the general public. Clinical psychology, from its beginning, has focused on *rooting out individual pathology*. Freudians believed the avenue for this was in exploring the subconscious. Decades later, the behavioral revolution suggested that symptoms could be formed and resolved through learned systems of rewards and punishments. Cognitive psychologists successfully pushed back, arguing that our rich internal worlds govern behavior and are open to change. More recently, postmodernists have argued that pathology is a social construct developed through the use of language. Within each of these eras of psychology, the proposed mechanism of change has differed, but the underlying goal of identifying and rooting out individual pathology has not. Psychology has benefited from the influence of the other professions, and has certainly had a great amount of influence on each of them; many early family therapists and counselors were originally trained as psychologists.

In the US, social work emerged as a distinct profession in the early 1900s, serving the needs of the poor. While *clinical* social workers today focus largely on mental health care, the social work profession more broadly still reflects its roots as a profession of service to the poor and the suffering. Social workers have a much stronger history than the other mental health professions when it comes to confronting large-scale social problems like homelessness and racism. *LCSWs are likely to approach mental health care as fundamentally a resource issue,* helping clients gather and improve their internal strengths, family and social support, and community resources to overcome their mental and emotional struggles.

A few decades later, a number of therapists operating in different disciplines – communications, psychiatry, social work, and pastoral counseling, among others – developed similar ideas about how couple and family dynamics can influence individual functioning. Most notably, early family therapists observed that when patients were discharged from hospitals after treatment for mental illness, those who were released to their families needed to be re-hospitalized earlier and more often than those who had been released to live on their own. This led to the development of the field now called marriage and family therapy. Though its roots stretch back far earlier, it is generally agreed that family therapy as a distinct profession emerged in the 1950s, with state licensure for family therapists starting in the 1960s. *LMFTs typically perceive mental illness and mental health treatment as relational processes.* They work with individuals, couples, and families to strengthen relationships, so that these relationships are helpful in coping with or eliminating mental and emotional struggles rather than simply reinforcing them.

Around the same time, professional counseling sprouted in part from the career and school counseling fields, which themselves had emerged from the progressive guidance movement of the early 20th century. Counselors do indeed focus on wellness, career development, and client empowerment more than the other mental health professions do, and that particular focus on empowerment is a key reason why counselors define their work broadly. *LPCs view mental health treatment as a process of empowerment, where the counselor helps the client to choose and achieve the goals they set for themselves.* As the profession defines itself, counseling "empowers diverse individuals, families, and groups to accomplish mental health, wellness, education, and career goals."[44]

Today, each of these four professions is licensed in each of the 50 US states and the District of Columbia. Members of each profession are fully qualified to independently assess, diagnose, and treat mental illness. Indeed, this is a major source of both public and professional confusion about the differences between the professions: Since we're all qualified to do psychotherapy, and we often work side-by-side doing many of the same job functions, the differences may at first appear to be academic.

Hopefully, however, you see here how each profession has a different perspective on mental illness and the process of healing from it. Each approach is effective, and research routinely shows little to no difference in the effectiveness of different types of mental health professionals for treating common mental health diagnoses.[45] But each profession has a distinct history, a distinct (or at least partly distinct) set of skills, and a distinct body of knowledge supporting its unique perspective.

Perhaps more importantly, each profession reflects a different set of values that is deeply woven in the profession's history. Psychologists have a long tradition of placing high value on the scientific and intellectual understanding of pathology. Social workers have a long tradition of placing high value on serving the underserved and promoting social justice. Family therapists have a long history of placing high value on family relationships and prioritizing action over understanding. And counselors have a long tradition of placing high value on personal development and wellness allowing for the achievement of one's fullest potential.

These differences in values matter.[46] Different types of therapists work best together when their perspectives are different – when putting us together in a workplace is more like putting ingredients into a salad than a blender. There are great opportunities for collaboration between the professions, but also natural tensions that exist for good reason: LPCs and LCSWs *should* fight about the usefulness of pursuing personal happiness and achievement (an LPC value) when weighed against the social injustices that hold the client back and will continue to exist no matter what the client may personally achieve (an LCSW value). *Both perspectives are good and are critically important, and they meaningfully differ.* When therapists are unwilling to have that argument – when we present clients the false notion that they can always have it both ways, or when we simply fail to hold to the values that drove the development of our fields – we willingly throw ourselves into the professional blender, becoming generalist psychotherapist mush.

It is hard to blame individual therapists – and particularly newer ones – for making this choice, though. The different values that led to the development of each different profession and fueled their growth are not emphasized in the professions' codes of ethics, which at this point are largely interchangeable. And (again, with the possible exception of social work), graduate classes in the histories of each profession tend to focus on the mechanics of those histories – key figures, dates, major developments – rather than the social needs and professional values that each new field sought to address.

# On being a good therapist

'When a profession itself is relatively undefined in the mind of the professional – as appears to often happen in mental health care – a natural consequence is that it can be hard for that professional to know what it means to be good at their job. Helping your clients reach their goals is certainly a fine standard, but if your clients are in hospitals, the goals you may have for them could simply be not to hurt or kill themselves.

Surely some therapists would define a good or successful therapist as simply someone able to make a living in the field. While there is some appeal to this, it also reduces our work to just its commercial component. It makes being a therapist (of any kind) not appreciably different than being a car or appliance salesman. It also reduces our primary function to that of a marketer. I've known some therapists who were able to remain in their positions because they were very skilled marketers, so skilled that they could make up for the frequent turnover in clients that came from them not being all that effective at actually working with people.

### Who do we serve?

Therapists of all stripes have a number of stakeholders – people with a vested interest in the outcome of our cases, on an individual and collective level. Most easily and directly, our clients want to get better (at least most of the time); when therapy helps them do so, they walk away not just with immediate symptom improvement but with an improved long-term prognosis. Many studies have demonstrated that psychotherapy has a so-called "offset effect," where the immediate costs of therapy are more than offset by reductions in the average therapy client's medical costs in the months or years after therapy ends.[47] Therapy, in other words, makes them both healthier and wealthier.

Immediate family members also benefit when therapy goes well. When a client becomes healthier and more functional, their children, spouse or partner, family, and others are likely to do better as well. A non-depressed parent is a more present and effective parent than a depressed one, after all, and as family therapists like me are quick to note, one reason children act out can be to draw attention to problems with their parents. The benefits to others that come when an individual is in therapy are sometimes referred to as "spider effects" – tough to measure, but important nonetheless.

Finally, the community at large benefits when its members have access to, and make use of, mental health services. Those offset effects noted above can keep insurance costs down for everyone in an insurance company's care, providing a sort of financial reward to the community when therapy is going well. People struggling with symptoms of mental illness also miss many more work days than their neighbors without such struggles, and it would sensibly follow that they face more difficulty meaningfully contributing to their religious groups, charities, even recreational sports teams. Simply put, a community functions better when its residents are more mentally well.

This large group of stakeholders also includes other therapists. Every time one of our clients succeeds in therapy, they come away trusting the therapy process and those who provide it more than they did before. They are understandably more likely to recommend therapy to friends or colleagues, often recommending their own therapist just as they would with doctors or barbers or any other professional with whom they have had a positive experience. When therapy works – as it usually does – it helps our colleagues as well as ourselves.

With such a large group of people with a vested interest in the outcome of therapy, it at first seems simple that we should do our best work with our clients to help them reach their goals, and if we succeed in doing so, everyone will win. We make money, while payors (clients or their insurers, whoever is paying for therapy) save money in the long run; families and communities run more efficiently and effectively; and the whole field of psychotherapy earns new converts.

Unfortunately, it isn't always so simple.

Much as we would like to believe that every difficult choice in therapy is a false dichotomy, and that every conflict has a potential "win-win" solution, there are times when we are forced to choose the immediate needs of one person or group over another. This is perhaps easiest when one of those people or groups is in the room with us, while the other is not. But even in these instances, it is a mistake to presume we can effectively serve everyone's needs all of the time.

As one example, let's go back to Lex and Annalee, the couple we met at the beginning of this chapter. Research offers conflicting findings as to whether it would be better for the kids if the parents in a marriage like theirs split up; in either instance, the kids are likely to suffer. We as therapists might rightly argue that over the long term, therapy *can* bring happiness and stability to the family if Lex chooses to stay; what we cannot do is guarantee that it *will*. Perhaps more to the point, individual therapists will vary widely in the degree to which they support Lex's desire to leave versus nudging him to stay and work on the relationship.[48] This leads to public confusion: Are *family therapists* really working to support a notion of *family* any more so than any other kind of therapist?

A similar question can be applied to clinical social workers, whose history suggests they would be more oriented toward the well-being of the community than the other psychotherapy professions. But to an outsider, it can be virtually impossible to translate this into an expectation for anything different to happen in the therapy room. None of the therapy professions makes clear to incoming professionals how their values should be different from those of other mental health professionals.

## The costs of leaving this undefined

Consider the following questions. For each one, you probably have a clear answer for yourself. But for the moment, ignore your individual preference, and consider whether your *profession* offers any guidance on these questions. What would you say in response to each of these if you were answering as a representative of your mental health profession? No cop-outs here; if you say "it depends," you have to follow that up with what it depends on.

- Which is more important, achieving happiness or fulfilling responsibilities?
- Should parents be expected to put their children's needs above their own?
- Does low-level suffering, when it is not interfering with work or social relationships, warrant treatment?
- What elements of culture do not deserve respect?
- When is it appropriate to leave a job or relationship?

Your answers, on behalf of your profession, were probably middling. And with good reasons: The professions themselves don't provide answers to these questions.

If you want advice on diet, you go to a nutritionist. You may not like what they have to say, but you generally know that they stand for healthy eating habits. If you want advice on spiritual matters, you might go to a pastor, rabbi, or other religious official. Again, you may not like what they will have to say, but you know that the guidance they will give you will align with a specific set of values, based in the religion.

Psychotherapists offer no such inspiration for our work. We say we offer mental health and wellness, and that we can facilitate positive behavior change. But we don't make clear to the public what it is that we value and honor, or even what we believe a healthier life looks like. Considering the wide variety of philosophies and methods of therapy, the public should be forgiven – perhaps even applauded – for being skeptical of therapists promising to make their lives better, while also leaving "better" conspicuously undefined.

# Where to go from here

Clarifying our purpose and values would go a long way to restoring public trust in the field of psychotherapy. A meaningful period of soul-searching among professional leaders, returning to the very foundational questions that led the various mental health professions to be formed in the first place, is undoubtedly necessary for this to happen. I talk later in this book about a need for us to increase our acceptance of accountability; better defining our purpose and values should help sort out the question of to whom, exactly, we should be accountable.

It is worth noting that this is one task where the field of psychotherapy might actually be well-served by different answers coming from each of its respective professions. For example, social workers may embrace a purpose and set of values that is more geared toward community well-being. Their code of ethics already leans in this direction, relative to the other mental health professions. Marriage and family therapists, meanwhile, may prefer values more geared toward family and child well-being. Once better defined, these differences should be meaningfully instituted and enforced; MFTs could institute requirements for training or even for ethical practice that involve understanding and working with clients' perceptions of their *obligations* to their family, rather than focusing exclusively on their personal desires, especially when these two are incompatible.[49]

# Clarifying values will mean taking losses

We are witnessing the beginnings of this process in the skirmish over so-called "reparative therapy," which you may know as "conversion therapy" or "ex-gay therapy." Popularized by Joseph Nicolosi, it involves the use of psychotherapeutic techniques to change someone's sexual orientation from gay to straight. There is no evidence that this form of therapy is generally effective, though there are certainly anecdotal accounts. There are also many anecdotal accounts of significant harm done by the approach, particularly to children forced into treatment by their parents.

The practice of reparative therapy with minors has been banned in California, New Jersey, Oregon, and the District of Columbia, with several other states considering similar legislation. As of this writing, California's ban had survived court challenges all the way to the US Supreme Court, and it appeared likely that the New Jersey ban, which uses similar language, would also survive.[50]

As California and New Jersey enacted their bans, some practitioners of reparative therapy – many of whom had been based in California – either shut their doors, switched to an unlicensed profession like life coaching, or moved to another state. For all intents and purposes, they chose to leave their licensed professional group rather than conforming their practices to the newly defined standards for that group.

I would say that's a good thing.

One of the side effects of clarifying professional standards and intentions is that some practitioners will see that they fall outside of them. Therapists in this circumstance can either (1) change their way of working to fit into the newly clarified framework for their profession, (2) try to convince their professional group to find ways to include them, or (3) accept the difference between themselves and the standards of the group, and leave the group. To do otherwise risks being more forcefully drummed out, and potentially being exposed to lawsuits from clients in the meantime.

When a profession adopts clear professional standards and expectations, some therapists have to make this difficult choice. Professions will take losses, in at least small numbers, any time they better define themselves. That cost, I would argue, is far outweighed by the benefits to the public and the professions that come from having titles that actually mean something.[51]

# Money where our mouths are

Our professional associations in mental health are losing members and expressing concern about their long-term viability.[52]

Organizations like the American Academy of Pediatrics regularly publish reports to educate the public on issues related to children's medical health, from nutrition in school lunches to the impact of violence in media. While these reports are sometimes controversial, at the very least they show that the groups behind them have a core set of values that they believe in and act upon.

This was, at one time, a primary function of professional associations in health care: To speak to the public with a singular voice, from the knowledge and expertise of the profession, to broadly improve public health. This was part of the public trust bestowed upon professionals in all categories: In exchange for higher pay, professional stature, and general freedom from government intrusion into professional matters, any profession is expected to govern itself and offer meaningful public benefit. Providing clear, digestible public guidance on issues of present concern is an excellent way to reinforce that trust as being well-placed.

The psychotherapy professions have not done so well in this area. The APA and NASW put out occasional reports for public consumption, but they, like all of the mental health professional associations, seem to dedicate much more time and effort to lobbying legislators for greater recognition and reimbursement. "Public education" efforts from these organizations often take the form of brochures that individual members can use to help market their practices, rather than unbiased information that the public can do with as they see fit. In short, the associations tend to give the appearance that their primary value is survival, their primary interest a selfish one. To be sure, lobbying for insurance and Medicare reimbursement for services has public benefits, increasing access to mental health care, but it is clear that the associations are primarily after job security and improved pay for their own members.

Consider this: When was the last time a report from an association in a mental health profession, issued for the benefit of the public, really made waves? There have been a few controversial and widely discussed association reports over the past few years, but many of these were developed primarily for the purpose of internal decision-making for the association and not public education on key mental health issues. I've taken two of the major mental health professional associations, ACA and AAMFT, and reviewed their web sites to see whether they issued any reports to the public of any significance in recent years. Not only have they not, but if you approach these sites through the eyes of Jane Public, someone who simply wants to learn a bit about what professionals suggest are best ways for her to promote mental health in herself and her family, you will find little to help you.

ACA's site is clearly geared toward members and potential members. There's a find-a-counselor directory there for the public, but that really exists so that it can be advertised as a free member benefit (like all therapists, counselors have plenty of places where they can advertise). ACA's "Knowledge Center" is meant for counselors, not the public, and their "Publications" are not reports but books and other materials again for clinicians. *The public face of the national association for counselors shows little to no actual interest in the public.* AAMFT's is not much better; the home page consists primarily of information for therapists that the public would have little interest in – online continuing education for MFTs, an upcoming conference, job opportunities, and the like. Four clinical topics are given small spaces, with a brief introduction for each; these are AAMFT's "Therapy Topics," which do provide educational benefit for the public but are intended for therapists to use in brochure form as promotional tools. (Naturally, each one indicates that psychotherapy is an effective treatment option.) Again, the association's interest in the "public" looks more like an interest in how members can get the public's money.

Of course, none of these associations is run by mustache-twirling villains. (As you'll read later in this book, I still think you should join.) The associations are us – we collectively elect the leaders and ask them to represent us, we approve major organizational changes and changes to ethics codes by vote, and we have the power to force change when necessary. Indeed, the focus on member service above public education in these associations no doubt comes from elected leaders responding to members' anxieties about employment and income opportunities. Furthermore, the associations' web sites are by no means the only way the professions should be judged; they're just one specific public face.

But when professional associations in mental health all but ignore public concerns about mental health, and focus instead almost exclusively on that which will provide financial benefit to their members, the public slowly and understandably loses trust in the professions. It looks like we're more interested in bringing paying customers to our offices than we are in actually resolving mental health issues.

Even the American Psychiatric Association, an organization with a relatively strong public outreach arm, has faced increasing skepticism of its motives. The psychiatrists are in charge of the *Diagnostic and Statistical Manual of Mental Disorders* (DSM), which clinicians around the US rely on for diagnostic criteria and boundaries. Recent editions of the DSM have expanded the portion of the population that would qualify as having a mental illness at any given time, and the recent publication of the 5th edition of the DSM (DSM-5) was hastened along in part due to budgetary concerns. A number of critiques of the DSM and of psychiatry more generally have accused the American Psychiatric Association of being in the pocket of Big Pharma, and expanding diagnostic criteria so that psychiatrists and drug-makers can simply make more money.

Allen Frances, in his scathing critique of DSM-5 development, concluded that professional associations in mental health

> "have broken the faith. They seem inclined to protect only their members and their staff bureaucracies, showing little regard for the preservation of quality or upholding the interests of the public they are meant to serve. All of the mental health professional associations have remained remarkably passive in the face of massive drug overusage. None has raised much opposition to the recent false epidemics of childhood attention deficit disorder, autism, and bipolar disorder. Neutrality in these situations is not really neutral – it amounts to passive collaboration with bad diagnoses and inappropriate treatment. [...] Going with the flow of ever-expanding diagnostic inflation brings in more patients to treat and the chance for drug company subsidies."[53]

Perhaps the best illustration of professional associations' prioritizing themselves and their members above service to the public comes in the so-called Hoffman report, named for its lead author. This 2015 document was the result of an exhaustive independent investigation into the role of the APA in crafting policies that protected psychologists involved in the torture of military detainees.[54] According to the report, APA staff sought to curry favor with the Department of Defense (DoD) in hopes of expanding psychology's role in the military. They allowed DoD to pre-clear their ethics policies surrounding torture, so that APA guidelines would never be more restrictive than what DoD wanted. The APA protected psychologists who had been involved in torture. And while all this was occurring, the APA engaged in a communications strategy that was purposefully misleading to the public, claiming that they had strict and specific policies when in fact their policies were quite vague – and appeared to be intentionally so. While the fallout of the Hoffman report is likely to continue for some time, it shows the danger of allowing leaders of professional associations to determine for themselves what values they seek to uphold in their work.

If we are able to engage successfully in the task of clarifying our purpose and values as professions, we can be much more effective at focusing resources appropriately into tasks that promote those values. We can effectively collaborate on those projects that reflect shared values across professions, freeing each association from the need to independently reinvent the wheel. It's silly for each organization to have its own brochure for ADHD, for example, especially when each touts the benefits of psychotherapy and the science doesn't indicate that one type of therapist is any better than another type in delivering successful ADHD treatment.

Simply put, our job security will be better served if we can make it clear that we value more than our job security. To earn back the public trust we must return to the pursuit of a greater good that was promised by the initial development of each of the professions in mental health. These greater goods were a bit different for each profession, not just allowing but arguably *requiring* each new profession's formation and growth. While times have changed, the promise of each profession has not, and those values held by each group uniquely could, if more clearly stated, benefit students, professionals, and the public. The letters after our names could finally mean more than just the words they shorten; the titles could once again be meaningful.

# Early signs of progress

Any discussion of professional values can quickly get heated. To this day, the APA continues to face fierce internal criticism over its determination in 2009 that members should not be involved in military torture.[55] However, there has been some progress on the organization front, pushed ahead by passionate therapists coming together. Several organizations of therapists took formal actions in support of same-sex marriage before the

2015 Supreme Court ruling that made same-sex marriage legal nationwide. All of the major mental health associations have issued statements in opposition to therapies that claim to change one's sexual orientation. In California, a large, independent organization of family therapists has seen a wave of new leaders elected based on their commitment to making the organization more socially aware and active in public debate.[56]

It certainly takes effort, but remember that organizations of professionals are us. We elect the leaders and can be elected as leaders. We can push for the organizations to do better. Our involvement matters. There is a tension within associations, who want to maximize their membership and offer an inclusive umbrella; this can often run counter to making clear and specific values statements. However, this doesn't mean they are destined for inaction. One of the best examples of association activism I've seen occurred when one member pressed that same California organization to take a stance supporting same-sex marriage. The organization had expressed concern that it would lose members by taking any stance, whether supportive or opposed. That one member gathered survey data and statements from other members to make the case that *failing* to take a stand *would cost the organization even more members*.

Associations are us. They represent the profession. When the values of professionals evolve, the associations should reflect that evolution. Minority viewpoints deserve protection on many controversial issues, but there does come a tipping point where the profession – again, meaning us – has fundamentally shifted. We have to muster both the individual and collective courage to stand up against practices that have been shown to routinely do active harm or otherwise violate our professional values.

# Taking it personally: What you can do

You don't have to wait for your association to take a clearer stance on the nature of your work. On your own, you can define your place within your profession, and support clear and specific values in your work. These can make you much more attractive to prospective clients.

### 1. Know *your* purpose and values

Our professional values are meaningful, but as I've described here, they still leave clients unclear about who and what we're fighting for. The best and most immediate way to resolve this is for you to make clear to clients who and what you're fighting for. There are many different missions you can serve that are all well within the scope of your professional values – knowing who you are as an individual professional can help set you apart from other therapists.

Some authors advocate creating something of a personal mission statement, which I think is a good idea *as long as it is specific*. A mission of helping clients find better psychological health doesn't really say anything. A mission of protecting children does. A mission of helping clients live in accordance with their stated beliefs does. Indeed, helping clients pursue happiness and individual expression – to be one's authentic self – is a common and well-accepted mission in the field. A good, clear mission should drive many of the clinical decisions you make, and should set you apart from other therapists who have different missions and values.

This specific task does require a fair amount of self-awareness. It may even need to be accomplished through your own therapy, if you are sure you want to be a therapist but not clear on why that is. As you develop awareness of your own mission and values, be on the lookout for any areas of potential incompatibility with the values of the profession. While you can serve many different missions and values within your professional role, you do not have the freedom to go operate in a way that would be inconsistent with the core values of your profession.

## 2. Make your values clear to prospective clients

Once you have a clear sense of your specific purpose and values, share it with your clients. You may be surprised at just how much hunger there is for this. I'll give you an example from my own practice. I work primarily with couples, and for years I had a page on my web site describing the kind of work that I do. This was effective enough, as I've had a steady stream of clients and been able to build up a reasonable caseload each time I moved to a new city.

A few months ago as I was updating my site, I saw an opportunity to be more clear with clients about what I believe in. Rather than just talking about the services I offer, I changed my content to make it much more evident that *I believe in data-driven decision-making.* We can't always know the outcomes of major decisions in our lives – particularly the decision of whether to end a long-term relationship, or work to stay in it – but the more information we have to base the decision on, the better. I also don't believe in the pursuit of happiness over the pursuit of goodness; I believe that looking back on our lives with pride in old age often relies on enduring greater suffering in the short term. I am open with my clients that I do not believe that present-moment unhappiness, in and of itself, is reasonable grounds to end a long-term relationship, especially when there are children involved.

I included information on how I assess couples struggling with this difficult and emotional decision, providing them with data about their relationship and discussing its long-term impacts but not imposing a particular decision on them. I also added information about the scientific support for the model of therapy I use when working with those couples who have committed to doing all they can to heal their connection.

I got more inquiries from prospective new clients in the next month than I had in the past six.

When you stand for something, you quickly set yourself apart from other therapists in your community, even ones serving the same clientele. Clients are likely to feel more trust and confidence in you because you're being transparent about the values you hold. They will have a clearer sense of what to expect from you, which can reduce their anxiety in bringing you difficult material.

## 3. Walk the talk

Recall from the Introduction that media portrayals of psychotherapists are often negative, casting us as incompetent or unethical in our work. In order to counter the negative public perception that can result, we must stand up as individual therapists and get involved in public discussion and debate. As society's recognized experts in behavior change, we have a responsibility to be involved in such discussions, even when that means the discussion becomes a debate between therapists on different sides of the issue. When that happens, at least those in the position to make key decisions will be better informed about the arguments on both sides.

What it means to walk the talk necessarily depends on what the specific values are that you seek to uphold in your work. If you believe in community service, of course you can lower your fees for clients in need, but walking the talk may also mean that you launch a nonprofit organization where therapists in training provide similar services under your supervision. If you believe in strong workplace and other civil rights protections for people who identify as LGBT, in addition to serving this community in your practice you might also testify at local or state government hearings when such policies are being considered. In short, it helps us all when any one of us sees the work of psychotherapy as stretching beyond the walls of our office and into the larger community and society.[57]

# Task 2:
# Fix therapist training

Each of the psychotherapy professions works within an apprentice-ship model. Receive the classroom training you need, the philosophy goes, and sit at the foot of an expert for a few years, watching and learning what they do. After a certain time, you'll be prepared to work on your own.

This makes some intuitive sense in psychotherapy. There is general agreement that no amount of classroom learning can fully substitute for the experience of practicing therapy on your own. To learn how to do therapy, you need to see the subtleties of how a practicing therapist actually works with their clients, and your own early therapy work needs to be supervised. From mundane issues like how to have a conversation with a client about an unpaid balance, to sophisticated issues like how to conceptualize a difficult and complex case, working with someone who has been in the field for some time offers tremendous value to someone who is new to the work.

How much of this supervision is necessary before you are adequate-ly prepared to have your own practice? How can those senior to you really tell when you're ready?

These questions have become much more pointed in recent years, as graduate training has become more expensive and the internship hours nec-essary to achieve licensure have gotten harder to come by. Writing about the apprenticeship model in medicine, *Slate*'s Brian Palmer captured the same problem we now face in the therapy professions (I've taken the original quote and changed "physicians" and "doctors" to "therapists" here):

> "Over the past century, there have been additions to, but few sub-tractions from, the training process. [...] The long process doesn't just weed out the incompetent and the lazy from the potential pool of therapists — it deters students who can't pay for so many years of education or who need to make money quickly to support their families. That introduces a significant class bias into the therapist population, depriving a large proportion of the population of thera-pists who understand their background, values, and challenges."[58]

In other words, if you're poor, you're not likely to be able to be-come a therapist. In the absence of therapists from poor backgrounds, clients who are poor will have few therapists who deeply understand their strug-gles. And therapy will move closer to being a profession by and for the wealthy.

This is the state of therapist training today: A long and expensive process that often weeds out the wrong people, while allowing therapists of questionable skill and safety through to licensure. Increasing evidence suggests that many of the requirements to become a therapist don't serve their intended purposes. While efforts at fine-tuning requirements around curriculum and supervised hours are welcome, the psychotherapy professions are long overdue for a more expansive re-examination of how we bring newcomers into the field.

# Experience and effectiveness are not linked

We certainly all would agree that we want therapists to be adequately trained, but the definition of "adequate" seems to only get stricter over time. You could argue that we will continually need to add to graduate training as the knowledge base of the field expands, as it certainly has over time. If clinical effectiveness relies on absorbing that knowledge base, then of course training will have to get longer.

However, a growing body of research shows that clinical effectiveness doesn't improve with additional training. Really take that in for a moment: *Clinical effectiveness doesn't improve with additional training.* Several studies (Table 1) have tried and failed to find an overall difference in effectiveness between seasoned clinicians and newer ones. Many of these have involved not even brand-new graduates, who would have at least some level of experience, but rather graduate *students* who are often in their *very first year of doing therapy.*

---

## Clinical effectiveness doesn't improve with additional training.

---

*Table 1. A sampling of major studies that have tried and failed to link experience with effectiveness*

| Authors and year | Findings |
| --- | --- |
| Buckley, Newman, Kellett, & Beail, 2006 | Trainees in their first through third years of clinical experience were compared with clinical psychologists. Each group worked with 60 clients, who were matched between groups. Patients of both groups of clinicians significantly improved; no differences in treatment outcomes were found based on clinician experience level. |
| Okiishi, Lambert, Eggett, Nielsen, Dayton, & Vermeersch, 2006 | Outcomes were measured for more than 5,000 clients who had seen 71 therapists at a university counseling center. No differences in outcome were observed based on therapist experience (preinternship, internship, and postinternship therapists were compared). |
| Wierbicki & Pekarik, 1993 | In a meta-analysis of 125 studies examining premature dropout from therapy, neither therapist experience nor therapist degree type had any meaningful impact on dropout. |
| Shapiro & Shapiro, 1982 | In a meta-analysis of 145 outcome studies involving two or more types of treatment, therapist experience did not predict effect size once differences in study methodologies were accounted for. |
| Smith & Glass, 1977 | In a meta-analysis of 375 psychotherapy outcome studies, therapist experience only meaningfully correlated with client outcome for the small subset of studies of psychotic clients who received non-behavioral treatment. Even then, the correlation was quite low. |

It is worth noting that a minority of studies do find a correlation between experience and effectiveness.[59] However, there are two things about these studies that should give you pause: 1, studies have shown that when it comes to several specific treatment modalities, *any mental health training at all* can make someone more competent to deliver the service than community volunteers or self-help group leaders. The small subgroup of studies that does find a link with experience typically compare those with almost no experience to those with significant experience. A full graduate degree is almost certainly not a necessity for effectiveness when delivering a modern, manualized therapy.[60] And 2, the studies that show a link between experience and effectiveness commonly use a client's rating of the therapy – that is, their *satisfaction* with it – to determine effectiveness, rather than more objective measures of whether the treatment has actually worked. Even meta-analyses that seem to show strong connections between experience and effectiveness quickly crumble when this methodological flaw is accounted for.[61]

The graduate training and apprenticeship model in mental health is broken. We train students far longer than is likely needed, and in ways that don't reflect what we now know about what makes therapists better. In this section, I'll outline a number of concerns around the education, supervised experience, and exam processes new therapists must go through to join the ranks of licensed mental health professionals.

# Education

Educational standards have risen significantly over time. In the 1960s, the educational requirement to become licensed as an LCSW or MFT was typically a 36-semester-unit graduate degree. As licensure expanded across the country, the knowledge bases of all mental health fields grew, and specific groups sought to ensure that therapists were well-trained to work with their specific problem or population. Training requirements were added, and over the 1980s and 1990s most states changed to 48-semester-unit minimums. (This was also the typical requirement for states adopting the newer LPC licensure at the time.) As has been the case in medicine, when new training requirements were added, typically none of the old ones were removed. That's partly an understandable reaction to a growing base of scientific literature, and possibly at least in part due to educators remaining wedded to outdated ideas and not wanting to remove material we're used to teaching from the required curriculum. Today, graduate programs in mental health at the master's level are transitioning to 60-unit requirements.

Psychologists have been a bit more effective than the other professions in rejecting additions to their training requirements. After all, when your profession already requires a doctorate, how much more adding can reasonably be done? But the field of psychology has not been completely immune to the "curriculum creep" that has infected the other professions.

According to American Psychological Association data, in the 1997-98 academic year, public and private PhD programs required an average of 90 and 81 semester units to graduate, respectively. PsyD programs required more units, at 104 and 116 on average ("average" here being the median, not the mean, among programs providing data).[62] Those unit numbers appear to be fairly steady. However, as will be discussed later in this chapter, APA-accredited programs have added a variety of new experience requirements to the academic degree – so much so that the various practica and internships required in an APA-accredited doctorate now typically add up to more than 3,000 hours of supervised experience even *without* a postdoctoral internship.

As the training requirements have increased, both these increased requirements and tuition inflation have made the training to become a therapist significantly more expensive than it was even a generation ago.

In the 1997-98 year, in-state students paid an average of $245 per unit in tuition and non-residents an average of $420 per unit to attend APA-accredited psychology programs. Ten years later, in-state students paid an average of $465 per unit, while non-residents paid an average of $789. Cumulative inflation over that 10-year span was just under 30%, but tuition costs in psychology had almost *doubled*. Similar cost increases were seen in this time throughout higher education in the US; the mental health professions are by no means unique in this. However, it is noteworthy that while tuition costs in general were increasing faster than inflation, the master's level mental health professions have *also* been making degree requirements higher, greatly compounding cost increases.

Here's one way to think about the changes. In 1985, master's level therapists typically needed a 36-unit master's degree to become licensed. Let's suppose that Emily wanted to become a clinical social worker back then, so she went to Normal Hypothetical University, where the cost of tuition happened to be $200 per unit. Emily would have paid a total of $7,200 in tuition to get the degree she needed to become an LCSW. If Hypothetical University has gone through the average US tuition inflation since then, today they are likely to be charging more than $600 per unit. Let's say Emily's daughter, Selena, who wants to become an LCSW in 2015, decides to go to her mother's alma mater to get the degree required now, which takes a minimum of 60 units. Selena's total tuition cost will be *more than $72,000.*

Of course, other prices have risen as well over the past 30 years; consumer prices have roughly doubled since 1985 due to inflation. But the cost of the education necessary to become a master's level therapist is more than *ten times* what it was 30 years ago.[63] In inflation-adjusted dollars, it costs more than five times as much to get a master's degree leading to psychotherapist licensure today than it did in 1985 (see Table 2). And that's just tuition. It leaves out other expenses, and the greater difficulty students now have obtaining financial aid. In professional schools, which now account for roughly a quarter of the APA-accredited psychology programs around the country, a majority of students receive no financial assistance whatsoever.[64]

*Table 2. Graduate tuition at a hypothetical master's degree program leading to therapist licensure, presuming tuition costs of $200 per unit in 1985 and average educational inflation since then, adjusted for inflation (in 2010 dollars)*

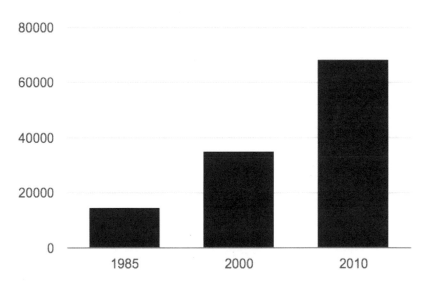

*Source data: Educational inflation data from Timothy McMahon available at http://inflationdata.com/Inflation/Inflation_Articles/Education_ Inflation.asp . These figures start from a 1985 per-unit tuition cost that is hypothetical, and extrapolate later figures from educational inflation data and changes in the unit requirements for master's degree programs (36 in 1985, 48 in 2000, 60 in 2010). The exact numbers are thus not especially meaningful, but the degree of growth is. Figures here are adjusted for regular (i.e., non-education) inflation using the Consumer Price Index calculator at http://www.usinflationcalculator.com .*

The combined factors of increased training requirements (largely at the master's level), tuition costs rising much faster than inflation in the rest of the economy, and decreases in the amount of financial aid available to graduate students, have created an environment where most students need to borrow large sums of money to even attend graduate school. Their salaries upon graduation – and remember that graduation occurs years before licensure – may not be enough to sustain the graduate and their family.

Across professions (though excluding degrees in medical fields, law, and theology), those who complete doctoral degrees using any borrowing at all have an average debt load of almost $80,000, almost three-fourths of which comes from their graduate education. Those who borrow to complete master's degrees graduate with an average of more than $50,000 in debt.[65] Remember, too, that this is just the *principal*, or the amount borrowed – repaying a $50,000 debt on a 10-year schedule at 6.8% interest will actually require almost $70,000 in total payments.[66]

Though those are big numbers, you might understandably ask: How much debt is actually a problem? So long as our salaries allow us to make the monthly payments on our educational debt, does it really matter what the total numbers are?

In short, the salaries of many new professionals in psychotherapy don't allow them to make the monthly payments on their debt. Many therapists in my generation refinanced student loan debt at rates around 2%. Current student loan financing is usually at interest rates of 5% to 7%,[67] and consolidation loans have an interest rate determined by a weighted average of existing loans. That may not sound like much of a difference at first, but over the life of a $100,000 debt refinanced into a 30-year repayment schedule, the difference between a 2% rate and a 5% rate is more than $60,000. The web site FinAid, set up as a public service to help students and their families obtain aid and calculate debt repayments, estimates that you need an annual salary of more than $64,000 to be able to afford repaying a $100,000 debt at a 5% rate over 30 years.[68]

Most master's-level therapists, and many Psychologists, simply don't make that much, especially when starting their careers. According to the federal Bureau of Labor Statistics, here are the median annual salaries for full-time work in the four major psychotherapy professions:[69]

*Table 3. 2014 median annual full-time salaries in psychotherapy professions*

| | |
|---|---|
| Clinical Psychology | $68,900 |
| Marriage and Family Therapy | $48,040 |
| Clinical Social Work | $41,380 |
| Professional Counseling | $40,850 |

*Source data: US Bureau of Labor Statistics.*[70]

As you can see, while the salaries for psychologists are significantly higher, they are the only professional group that requires a doctoral degree – and the added expense that comes with it. As noted above, the average psychology PsyD program is more than 100 semester units, compared to the 60 required at the master's level.

The effects of this on students have been significant. In terms of raw dollars, the cost of graduate education has of course increased significantly; at the same time, funding for student scholarships and even loans has become much more difficult to secure. These factors together mean that today it is much, much harder for a prospective therapist with a strong skill set and academic record, but few financial resources, to fulfill their dream of becoming licensed.

Educational debt is frequently mentioned as a key reason millennials are buying fewer cars and homes than prior generations.[71] Many millennials say that their student debt factored into decisions to delay getting married (29%) and having children (43%). It might also be leading otherwise well-qualified students who would like to be therapists into other careers: Almost a third of millennials said that student debt had considerable impact on their choice of career fields.[72] Among those who did go on to choose psychology, more than half of recent graduates said their educational debt led them to delay buying a home, and 46% said it led them to delay having children.[73]

Recent graduates of PsyD programs in psychology entering human service professions – that is, those going into clinical work, rather than research or consulting – now report a median of *$200,000 in student loan debt*.[74] More than 20% of all those with doctorates in psychology (PsyD or PhD, entering any career path) have debt loads of more than $160,000.[75] While hard numbers for the other professions are more challenging to come by, bear in mind that the average student borrower has racked up about $30,000 in debt before they even start graduate school.[76] It is reasonable to believe that total educational debt loads of more than $100,000 are becoming increasingly common among all therapists, with total debt loads of more than $200,000 becoming increasingly common among psychologists. According to the FinAid calculator, the median social work salary of $40,970 would only be sufficient to pay off a $63,000 debt over 30 years at 5% interest. Total payments on that debt would amount to more than $121,000.

A 2008 report on student debt among social workers begins with a simple and saddening quote from one of their survey participants:

> "Unmanageable debt, poor preparation in training for job negotiations, and low salaries in the social work profession make the social work profession untenable."[77]

That same report showed that nearly a third of social workers had to rely at least in part on credit cards to finance their education. In spite of a nationwide shortage of social workers, the report concluded, "educational debt is pushing people away" from the profession. It seems likely that the same is true for counselors, family therapists, and psychologists.

Despite all of this data, responses to the educational debt crisis in mental health have been underwhelming. That there is a problem here is fairly well-known, and as I hope you would agree after reading the past few pages, easy to establish. But rather than making a concerted effort to reduce educational or licensing requirements – the most direct and meaningful path to easing the financial burdens on incoming professionals – the professions have responded instead with efforts at student loan reimbursement plans and funded internships, generally tied to public service and awarded to only a tiny fraction of those who desperately need (and would qualify for) them.

Universities understandably appreciate these types of solutions, as they don't have to worry about addressing excesses in their curriculum or staffing, they don't need to find ways to reduce exorbitant tuition rates, and they can correctly advertise to worried students that brand new programs are available to help with their loan burden after they graduate (the overwhelming majority of graduates will not actually receive these awards).

For the professions to continue to place this heavy burden on their newest and most vulnerable members is unconscionable. And when it comes to the financial strains new therapists face, their student loans are quite literally only the beginning.

# Supervised experience

The apprenticeship model of therapist training dates to the early days of psychology as we know it. Freud's followers studied under him for years before branching out on their own, as did Jung's – and Jung had once been a student of Freud. As the ranks of early psychoanalysts grew, the custom was to be in therapy as a subject of analysis while you were also seeing your own cases. This worked to ensure that you understood yourself and the process of being a client. To this day, many graduate programs in the mental health professions either require or strongly encourage their students to go to therapy as a patient, regardless of whether the student actually has any mental or emotional problems.[78]

---

## For the professions to continue to place this heavy burden on their newest and most vulnerable members is unconscionable.

---

Of course, for those who were developing their skills as therapists and were attending therapy at the same time, the temptation to use their own therapy as a place for talking about their cases was simply too great. That makes sense: As you are starting out as a therapist, you naturally want support and confirmation that you're doing well (or at least well enough), and you want to consult with an expert therapist on cases that you're struggling with. If you're already meeting regularly with an expert therapist, wouldn't you use the time for some case consultation?

Newer therapists did so with regularity, to the frustration of their more seasoned therapists – who wanted to do more intensive analytic work on the patient in front of them, and did not want to waste time discussing the patient's patients. The more experienced analysts got tired of hearing about their clients' cases, and wanted to separate case discussion (or, as we now call it, supervision) from therapy. That way they could focus on doing therapy and leave the supervision to someone else. So, as experienced psychoanalysts gathered to set early supervision standards for the field, they rather arbitrarily decided on two years as the amount of time one should practice under supervision before being allowed to practice independently.[79] That length of time (many states quantify it today as 3,000 hours of experience, or thereabouts) was published *in 1924*, and has stuck in the mental health world now for almost 100 years.

It may help to understand what was happening around that time in other advanced professions: Namely, too many people were entering them. Medicine is the best example; a 1910 report declared that the US suffered from a tremendous *over*production of doctors, and needed to raise training requirements not so much to improve clinical care as to reduce the number of new doctors.[80] The report was advocating the creation of hoops for new professionals to jump through *simply for the hoops' own sake*, to keep doctors' incomes high and their profession exclusive.

The training requirements for today's psychotherapists appear to have been constructed as much from naïveté as cynical self-interest, although based on the era, it is reasonable to suspect that early supervision requirements were as much about keeping psychology exclusive as they were about ensuring practitioner effectiveness. As other mental health professions including clinical social work, marriage and family therapy, and professional counseling have emerged in the decades that followed, these new professions have sought state licenses that would also allow them to practice psychotherapy, but with less academic training than psychologists receive. (All states require doctoral degrees, which typically take four to five years to complete, for licensure in psychology. Master's degrees are required for the other professions and are significantly shorter, often completed in just two or three years.) Psychologists, for understandable reasons, were concerned about the emergence of these master's-level therapists. Their field operated under the assumption that less training simply wasn't adequate for safe and effective clinical practice. Psychotherapy, they argued, was a craft, and if performed poorly, it could actually be quite damaging to a patient's mental health.[81]

These arguments have faded over time, but haven't disappeared. It was only in 2009 that professional counseling and family therapy completed the task of achieving licensure laws in all 50 states of the US. As these newer professions worked year after year, and state after state, toward this goal, it was common for psychologists to oppose MFT and LPC licensure bills on the grounds that the master's level professions had scopes of practice that were too broad given their lesser training. In order to achieve licensure, the master's-level professions fought to avoid psychology's doctoral-level educational requirements, but compromised by adopting essentially the same standard for apprenticeship that psychologists had been using: 3,000 hours, or roughly two years of full-time supervised experience. The tradition in psychology thus permeated the other professions without ever being subjected to meaningful critical examination.

Today, most states in the US still use something close to the two-year standard for both psychology and the master's-level mental health professions. It varies a bit from state to state and license to license, but 3,000 hours of experience or thereabouts is the norm. However, there is little to no evidence that two years of supervision time is better than one year or worse than three, and surprisingly little evidence that supervision actually impacts the quality of client care *at all*. Two years is a long time to ask new professionals, with significant student debt loads, to work at reduced wages before they can practice independently – especially when there isn't any demonstrable benefit of keeping a supervisor over them for so long.

## Employed-ish: Life as an intern

Most people associate the term "internship" with schooling, as well they should: internship programs around the world provide tremendous educational opportunity for students who are seeking to learn practical skills in addition to the academic training they're getting at the same time. While internships have always had something of a dark underbelly – it's tempting, as an employer, to seek ways to replace low-wage workers with *no*-wage workers by recasting their positions as "internships" – mental health care has been especially hard on the very concept of an internship.

For psychologists, there is both a pre-doctoral internship and a post-doctoral internship in most states. The pre-doctoral internship is, at best, mildly academic: Students at this stage are in their "internship year," are not attending classes, and are often working in internship sites hundreds or even thousands of miles away from the graduate programs where they are enrolled. The program ostensibly monitors the student's progress, but from such a distance, this often means nothing more than having the supervisor at the internship site fill out a form every so often, notifying the university of any serious concerns. That said, psychologists have an advantage over the other mental health professions, in that many of their internships are paid.

They often aren't paid *well*, mind you, especially given the burden many interns take on of moving across the country and away from their loved ones for a year so that they can complete their degree at an accredited internship. But they are paid, with a median stipend of $22,776 as of 2014.[82] Those interns who aren't able to find an accredited internship – and there are many, given the chronic shortage of accredited psychology internships[83] – often report they are willing to work in unpaid internships if necessary.[84] This could be seen as a mark of desperation to get the internship done and advance in one's career, or it could be seen as a relative lack of concern over pay among some still in the midst of their education.

Of course, while students are in school, they may be able to obtain additional financial support, through their universities and through added student loans if necessary. There is a far greater problem, and that's what happens to students in the mental health professions *after* they graduate. To start with, most new graduates are far from done with the title of "intern."

For psychologists, most states still require a post-doctoral internship. This position is supervised by a licensed professional, but is not under the auspices of any educational setting (since the intern has already graduated). Typically, a post-doctoral internship in psychology is another 1,500 hours they will have to put in before they can get licensed to practice independently. While there isn't especially good data on how much postdoc interns in psychology make in salary, many jobs appear to pay between $30,000 and $50,000 for the year.[85]

In the master's level professions, the issues are similar but the titles can vary from state to state. This gets confusing for everyone involved, including students, universities, employers, policymakers, and clients. If you're a master's-level psychotherapist who has completed your degree program but not yet attained the experience and passed the exams for full licensure, you need to work under the supervision of a licensed therapist. During that time, you might be designated by your state as an "intern," an "associate," someone working under a "limited license," or something different entirely.

Whatever the title is, the time between graduation and licensure is a challenging phase in professional development for many, as they have to begin repaying their student loans while making relatively low salaries. The pressure to complete required hours of experience for licensure so that one can move on to the next career stage creates an environment ripe for exploitation by workplaces and supervisors who see these new professionals as low-cost labor. But the biggest problems can come for those who are designated by their states as "interns." This title invites employers to call the positions they will be hiring such professionals into "internships," and even well-meaning employers can often think that anything called an internship can be – or is even *supposed to be* – unpaid.

If you are a new therapist working in an "internship" without pay, it is for a non-profit whose cause you believe in and want to support, and you can do so without causing undue strain on your own financial situation, more power to you. There are many non-profits who need your help and will fall over themselves to tell you how much they appreciate your contributions.

On the other hand, if you have completed your graduate degree and are working in an "internship" in a for-profit setting, there is a very good chance your employer is violating federal law.

The federal Department of Labor is tasked with enforcing federal labor laws, including limits on how for-profit employers can make use of unpaid interns. In brief, for an unpaid internship to be legal in a for-profit setting, it has to meet all six of these criteria:[86]

1. **It has to be similar to training that would be given in an educational environment.** It's tough to determine whether mental health internships would meet this standard, since many of them specifically require that the therapist have already graduated from their educational setting. But we can set this aside, as this criterion is hardly the biggest problem on this list for employers.

2. **It has to be for the benefit of the intern.** Again a tough call; the intern benefits by gaining hours of experience toward licensure, but the deck is stacked against them – they have to get those hours somewhere. Still, the hours are a quantifiable benefit, so we can presume that unpaid internships in mental health are within this standard.

3. **The intern must not be entitled to a job at the end of the internship.** This one's easy enough; most employers make that perfectly clear in their intern contracts. No problems here.

4. **The employer and the intern understand that the intern is not entitled to wages for their time in the internship.** Again, easy enough – this is typically included in the contract.

5. **The intern must not displace regular employees, but instead work under the close supervision of existing staff.** And here's where things get sketchy. While it is true that the interns are working under the supervision of licensees at the site, here in California it isn't terribly unusual for a site to have just one or

two supervisors and a dozen or more interns – enough that if the unpaid interns weren't there, the site would not be able to provide services to all of its clients because they wouldn't have the manpower. That, to me, sounds like the very definition of displacing regular employees.

6. **The employer must get no immediate advantage from the activities of the intern, who may even occasionally impede the operations of the employer.** This is an even clearer problem among for-profit businesses hiring unpaid interns in mental health. Any site getting paid for the services provided by unpaid interns should read this with concern. Money is a pretty clear and immediate advantage.

Those rules, again, apply most clearly to for-profit businesses; nonprofits and government settings, where a great many "interns" in mental health are volunteering, have somewhat different rules.[87] But both nonprofits and for-profits benefit financially when new graduates put themselves through the struggle of an unpaid position simply so they can gain hours of experience toward licensure. And there is at least one instance of a state labor board applying these standards to a non-profit setting: The University of California San Francisco (UCSF) employed a post-doctoral psychology intern in a stipend position at 17 hours a week, with the stipulation that hours worked beyond that were on a volunteer basis. However, since she was routinely required to work 50-hour weeks in the position, the California labor board awarded her several thousand dollars in back wages, damages, and interest. They determined that because UCSF wasn't linked to her academic program (criteria 1), UCSF received a clear benefit from her presence (criteria 6), and having her as an intern allowed UCSF to not hire other staff to conduct the same clinical work (criteria 5), it was not legal for UCSF to claim that she was participating in an unpaid internship. They needed to pay her at least minimum wage as an employee for all the hours she worked.[88]

The message from the labor board was clear: Non-profits and government settings are not automatically excluded from wage and hour laws. However, many nonprofits continue to use mental health professionals who have completed their academic degrees in positions they call "internships." These positions often pay nothing.

## High standards don't equal high salaries

When I've talked about internship and debt issues with other mental health professionals, I usually see some sense of surprise and relief on their faces. They're surprised that the problems related to debt and licensure really are quantifiably worse than a generation ago, and relieved to know that they aren't the only ones worried for the new generation of therapists (which sometimes means being worried for themselves and their families).

Other audiences sometimes react more skeptically, though. With graduate degrees, surely all of us are on career paths that may be rough at the beginning, but get better with time, right? If it were easy, as the saying goes, everyone would be doing it. Aren't we actually well-served by the process of education and licensure needed to become a mental health professional being highly difficult?

The short answer to this question is no. Neither students nor professionals nor the public are well-served by a training process that rewards wealth rather than skill. The longer answer is that the benefits that a difficult system theoretically should bring – upward pressure on wages and higher respect for mental health work – aren't happening.

I mentioned wages earlier, and the numbers bear repeating here. Between 2001 and 2009, psychologists who were direct service providers saw their salaries *decrease* by about 20% in inflation-adjusted dollars. For the master's level professions, their salaries rose about 10% between 2007 and 2013 in raw dollars. But inflation rose 12.4% in that same time frame, meaning that the real purchasing power of normal salaries is declining for master's level therapists, while the debt situation is significantly worsening.

Even with wages and debt loads as they are, a skeptic might argue that increasing debt and stagnant wages are simply "market corrections." In essence, they are saying that the market is becoming more efficient at pricing education and mental health services closer to their actual value. When an increasing number of people want mental health licenses, and the number of people going to psychotherapy is flat or declining (and those who do go are coming for fewer sessions), *of course* wages aren't going to rise. From a strictly free-market perspective, they shouldn't. Skeptics also will note that the $67,760 average salary for psychologists is enough to pay off more than $105,000 in debt without financial difficulty.[89]

That argument would make sense if wages and debt correlated on an individual level (that is, if those who made the most also were those with the highest debt loads). If that were the case, it would just be griping when we talk about higher costs of education and stagnant salaries; it would be true that most psychologists simply would pay off those debts over time.

Unfortunately, we know that this isn't the case. Across professions, those who take on the greatest debt are often those who will be *least* equipped to repay it. Consider the plight of a student from a low-income neighborhood. She wants to get her psychology degree and license so that she can help those in her neighborhood who desperately need intensive mental health services. Because her high school is less likely to be strong, she will have greater difficulty getting into a good and low-cost college. So she's likely to have significant student debt before even starting graduate school. If her undergraduate grades were good, she may be able to get into a lower-cost graduate school, but if not, her debt will only balloon over five more years of education. When she finally returns to her neighborhood to provide the services she set out to provide, she's likely to find that working in an outpatient or residential setting there will only hold her wages down; the salary averages for psychologists are bumped up by those who work in hospitals, employment services (occupational testing), and scientific positions. She's likely to make just $54,000 a year in a residential care facility.[90]

So what do we tell an aspiring psychologist who wants to provide services to underserved communities? Tough luck?

## Leaving the field

In California, therapists in the master's level professions must register with the state upon completion of their graduate programs. They remain registered as interns or associates (the title varies depending on the specific profession) until they complete their required experience and exams for licensure. In 2010, Sean O'Connor, then an employee with California's licensing board, found that as many as a third of the family therapists and social workers who registered with the state in a given year would never make it to their licensing exams. (Educational psychologists were not part of the analysis, and counselors did not yet have licensure in the state.) This represented a major concern to the licensing board, and it should have represented a serious concern to taxpayers as well – many of the state's therapists come from publicly subsidized graduate programs, and even many who go to private schools receive loan funding that comes in part from public sources.

O'Connor looked at licensing data and conducted a survey of registrants to find out what kept them from getting through the process.[91] He examined an impressively broad range of factors, analyzing each of them in isolation as well as in combination with the others. What he found was disheartening for those who would like the therapy field to be an achievable dream for diverse populations: Among the strongest factors decreasing the likelihood that someone would get through to licensure were race, with African-Americans and Latinos far less likely to get licensed, and time spent completing licensure requirements while raising a child.

In plain English, if you're poor, if you're of Latino or African-American descent, or if you have family obligations, at this point in time it is incredibly difficult to become a therapist. And none of those things have anything to do with how talented a therapist you might be.

## Research on supervised experience

There is surprisingly little research about what makes supervision effective, and as noted above, most of it is inconclusive at best. However, there is a great deal of research on what supervisees *like*. Why not just consider this research when determining how supervision should go, and organize the task around what the experience of supervisees over the years has been?

The problem with this idea is that what people *like* and what is actually *effective* can differ wildly. Research on education is the best example here: Students will give the best reviews to professors who are entertaining and teach to the test, making it easy for students to get good grades. Professors who produce better long-term learning are often less liked.[92]

We all like it when we are not inconvenienced. Hearing from a supervisor, even in a supportive manner, that you are deficient in a particular area of therapy and need to spend time getting better at it – then putting in the time and effort to do that – is a *major* inconvenience, one that you might even find embarrassing. The experience can shake your confidence. It's one that hopefully will make you a better therapist, but at the time, it is possible and even probable that you won't like it. You might *appreciate* it, but you probably will not *enjoy* it.

Sure enough, the research on how supervisees experience supervision reflects a strong desire to get better without being inconvenienced. Supervisees understandably dislike when supervisors miss or are late for supervision, or are openly disrespectful.[93] But supervisees also dislike supervisors who emphasize skill development,[94] supervisors who are seen as challenging,[95] and supervisors who take an instructive stance.[96] These findings all suggest the same conclusion: Supervisees don't like being pushed to improve.

I get that, and I bet you do too. No one enjoys hearing they're doing something wrong or poorly. It brings up anxiety about our ability to do good work, and perhaps even insecurity about our ability to help clients. But understanding where you need improvement is a necessary step to getting better. Otherwise, you'll be like the musician who simply keeps playing the same song over and over, missing the same notes each time, and never figuring out the more challenging chord transitions you need.

Many studies of supervision make the mistake of assuming that if supervisees *like* the supervision, or if the supervisee *describes* the supervision as helpful, then the supervision must be improving clinical outcomes.[97] In reality, efforts to determine the actual impact of supervision on client outcome have so far not produced strong results. What little research does exist on supervision enhancing clinical skill suggests that very few supervisory tasks improve therapist performance.[98] One that does is called *deliberate practice.*

In deliberate practice, therapists repeatedly practice a small skill that they are struggling with. This is no different from a musician practicing a difficult chord transition or a basketball player shooting hundreds of free throws. While this appears to produce reliable results in improving clinical outcomes, very few supervisors make it a regular part of supervision.[99]

## The gate that never closes

Even if supervision *couldn't* improve the effectiveness of prelicensed therapists – and for clarity, current research suggests it often *doesn't,* but also that it *could* – there's a worthwhile philosophical debate to be had about why therapists go through a period of supervision at all. If supervision in psychotherapy exists for the purpose of making therapists better, than it would certainly appear that we are largely failing new professionals in this work.

But supervision can be conceptualized from another framework as well: One of *monitoring.* From this stance, the supervisor's job is not, in fact, to make supervisees any more clinically effective in their work. Rather, it is to maintain a watchful eye over the supervisee's caseload to ensure that the supervisee is behaving legally and ethically, that they are responding to crises appropriately, and that they are generally not endangering their clients. From this perspective, the supervisor's responsibility is essentially one of *professional gatekeeping*. They should intervene when necessary to either retrain supervisees who are showing problematic behaviors, or in severe cases, counsel them out of the profession.

Of course, supervisors who see their role as making supervisees better also have this gatekeeping responsibility, and there is evidence that supervisors in general take this responsibility seriously.[100] However, there are few mechanisms to be used to effectively exercise this responsibility. As we will see with licensing exams momentarily, supervisors stop very few people from entering the psychotherapy profession. Our failure in this area (I say "our" as I'm a supervisor myself) means that unprofessional and even dangerous clinicians can slip through the internship stage and on to licensure, where there will be no supervisors to monitor their behavior and where their misdeeds can hurt the collective reputation of the field.

It is clear that supervisors want to stop some supervisees from becoming licensed, but have limited tools at their disposal to do so. Supervisors dealing with troubling behavior among supervisees will typically choose from the following actions:

**Informal advising.** Ideally, this would be all it would take to solve a problem of supervisee behavior. A quick conversation in a clinic hallway, or even a few minutes of individual supervision to ensure the supervisee understands why their behavior is troubling, can be a useful first line of intervention for more minor problems.

**Retraining.** This is a bit more formal, and may involve a defined improvement plan to which the supervisee agrees in writing. In clinic or hospital settings, this may involve the Human Resources department. Once the plan is in place, the supervisor is often expected to monitor the change in supervisee behavior to ensure the desired changes take place.

**Administrative shifts.** Supervisors may temporarily stop referring new clients to the problematic supervisee, require them to attend additional supervision, or even suspend them from clinical work.

**Reporting to licensure boards.** Supervisors appear to take this action only in extreme circumstances, and even then, only in situations where state law allows for such reporting and the possibility of such a report is clearly outlined in the supervisee's contract.

**Firing or dismissal.** Supervisors may determine that a supervisee's actions are so egregious that they can no longer trust the supervisee to work safely. In such cases, the supervisor refuses to expose themselves to the ongoing risk of working with that supervisee, and the supervisee is fired.

**Formal counseling out of the profession.** Supervisors may determine that a supervisee is unfit for the profession, and may formally guide the supervisee to consider other lines of work.

Obviously, these actions are not mutually exclusive. A supervisee might be fired and reported to the state licensure board in one fell swoop. Even so, while many of these actions are rightly described as severe, consider how little they do to actually *remove from the field* a new professional who is not fit for it. Firing a supervisee often just means they will find a new employer. Reports to licensing boards, even in the rare instances where they are actually made, may not be pursued by those boards if they don't have client permission to access the records they might need to establish a violation of professional standards. And formal counseling out of the profession is not binding on the supervisee. Especially given how much time and money the supervisee has already invested in building a career as a therapist, it may be unrealistic to expect a supervisee to take in the guidance of a more seasoned professional, cut their losses, and move to a different line of work.

Weighing the full scope of this section, supervision in the therapy professions appears to go on for far longer than necessary, without meaningfully improving therapists' skills, and only minimally serving a gatekeeping function. Supervision requirements keep poor and minority therapists out of the field while offering little, if any, measurable benefit to the professions or the clients we serve.

# Licensing exams

In addition to the education and experience one needs to become a therapist, we all must take licensing exams. Most mental health professions in most states now utilize national exams, which is helpful for license portability. National exams also improve efficiency (far better to have a single exam development process than 50 different ones testing on largely the same things) and keep the professions cohesive across state lines. Of course, laws on issues like child abuse reporting differ from state to state, so in addition to the national exam, most therapists wind up taking a state law and ethics exam on the road to licensure.

You might be surprised at how little good these exams actually do.

As with supervision, it is important to bear in mind their intended purpose. License exams do not assess your effectiveness as a therapist. They aren't meant to. That bears repeating: *License exams do not assess your effectiveness as a therapist.* They are a state licensing board's best effort at assessing whether you have the minimal knowledge (*not* skill, knowledge) to be able to practice independently without being a danger to the public. That's all. When therapists decry the fact that license exams are nothing like doing therapy, they're right – and their point isn't relevant. Exams aren't *supposed* to be like therapy. If you want to know how good you are as a therapist, look elsewhere, because exams are not *and are not intended to be* a barometer of clinical effectiveness. They are a somewhat crude assessment of safety for independent practice.

With that aim in mind, do they work? Do licensing exams make therapists safer?

There's remarkably little data to answer that question. We can't, at this point, randomly assign therapists to either exam or no-exam conditions to see whether one group would practice any more safely than another. We could look at consumer complaints to licensing boards, and see whether licensees (having passed their exams) had fewer complaints-per-therapist than those who are still under supervision. But that data, too, would be highly questionable; if it turns out that licensees have fewer complaints, is it because they have proven they knew the law (at least as it existed when they were tested)? Or, is it because they...

...have different clients who may be less likely to complain?
...are more likely to be working part time, and thus seeing fewer clients?
...are seeing higher-paying clients who know they can just go to a different therapist if the one they are seeing seems unethical?
...are less likely to work in clinics where information on filing ethical complaints is prominently displayed?

Each of those and many more possibilities come to mind. The exercise works just as well in the other direction, too. If it at first appears that interns or associates get *fewer* complaints than licensees, that could be because they're under close supervision. But it also could be for a wide variety of other reasons. And to take it a step further, higher numbers of consumer complaints wouldn't necessarily mean that any one group was actually practicing in a less safe manner than others; it could just mean that group's clients were more aware of the complaint process.

As you can see, it is quite difficult to determine through research whether license exams "weed out" therapists who are less safe than their peers. The exams do weed out some therapists, but as it turns out, they weed out very, very few. And they probably weed out the wrong ones.

---

## Licensing exams weed out very, very few. And they probably weed out the wrong ones.

---

### Almost everyone passes

California, my home state, is a good place to look at licensing exam statistics. For one thing, we have a lot of psychotherapists here: More than 75,000 under the governance of the state's Board of Psychology and Board of Behavioral Sciences (the BBS governs the master's level professions). For another, these boards are quite transparent about testing data.

To demonstrate how few examinees are actually "weeded out" by license exams, we'll use California's MFT Written Clinical Vignette test. In the first half of 2013, 992 people took the exam.[101] The overall pass rate for that six-month exam cycle was 82% (816 people passed). At first, that can appear to be an exam that is reasonably doing its job, weeding out almost one in five test takers. But a closer examination of the data – which, to the state's credit, is only possible because they make this level of data available to the public – shows that 86% of people taking the test *for the first time* passed it. 74% of those making their second attempt passed. And just over half (31 of 61) of those on their third attempt or higher passed the test. While there's some variability in pass rates from one six-month exam cycle to the next, those numbers appear to be pretty typical. They're also similar to the numbers for the state's vignette exam for LCSWs.

The fact that the pass rate goes down on subsequent attempts is good; if passing or failing were truly random, then the pass rate would stay the same from one attempt to the next. But notice what happens when we think about how candidates progress through this exam. More than 17 of every 20 examinees pass on their first attempt. About three quarters *of those who failed the first time* pass on their second try. And more than half *of the few still left* after two failed attempts get through on the third. The overall outcome of the exam process looks like Table 1 below.

Yes, some people do give up and drop out of the process along the way. Small numbers simply give up after failing, in some cases after failing just once. Others move out of state, for a variety of reasons, and seek licensure in their new home state. Still others exit the process for other reasons. This graph doesn't capture those dropouts – it only shows those who stay in the process – and by showing a single test cycle, isn't a perfect representation of the testing and retesting of a single cohort.[102] But those who drop out once they've made it to the testing process are a small group, and the graph gets the point across: Of those who stay in the exam process, *almost everyone* will eventually pass. Fewer than 1 in 50 will not.

And while the proportions differ, the same conclusion is true in all the mental health professions, among national exams as well as California's state exams: Hang in the testing process once you're in it, and you are *extremely* likely to pass. The pass rate for the EPPP, psychology's national exam, was 76% between August 2007 and July 2012.[103] The pass rate for the national Clinical Exam in social work was 79% in 2014.[104] For counseling, it's typically 78-80% on the National Counselor Exam, according to the National Board for Certified Counselors.[105] In each case, first-time test-takers perform better than those taking the exam a second or subsequent time (that's a good thing, from a test reliability perspective), so you can safely bump those numbers up several points for first-time examinees.

Ultimately, almost everyone passes. But what about those few who *don't* pass? Perhaps you know someone (or are someone) who failed at least one attempt at a licensing exam, and you've been wondering what meaning to put to that. Does failing an exam mean a psychotherapist is unsafe?

Probably not.

While we don't have any research on this question that is specific to mental health providers, studies of teachers and nurses have shown that license exams do not appear to improve the safety or effectiveness of a professional workforce. Instead, license exams appear to disproportionately shut out (1) people who identify as Hispanic and (2) people for whom English is not the language spoken at home.[106]

*Table 1. Examinee Outcomes for California MFT Written Clinical Vignette Exam Testing Process (based on January-June 2013 cycle)*

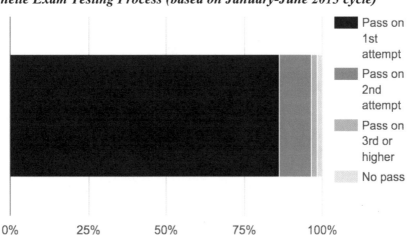

*Source data: California Board of Behavioral Sciences.*

The English language issue makes some sense, though that doesn't make it okay; it is easy to see how damaging this is to the profession. License exams are usually not offered in languages other than English, and require sophisticated vocabulary. States typically do not allow anyone, regardless of primary language, to bring in a translation dictionary to their test or to have extra time on the test. (States will typically make accommodations only for recognized disability, and being a non-native English speaker is not considered a disability.) So not only do non-native speakers need to process and correctly answer questions in a limited amount of time just like all other examinees, they also must frequently translate the question to their native language in their minds, develop a response, back-translate that response to English, and see how well it lines up with their available response choices.

Though those findings on license exams do come from other professions, and therefore should be taken with a grain of salt when considering how well they might apply to therapists, they should nonetheless be setting off alarms within the professions and within state licensing boards. There is no reason whatsoever to believe that those who identify as Hispanic or those whose native language is not English are inherently less safe as practitioners than non-Hispanic native-English-speakers. Furthermore, many states and the professions themselves are actively trying to improve the racial and ethnic diversity of the mental health professions, so that the populations we serve can have quick and easy access to professionals who understand their issues and concerns. If licensing exams don't appear to make us any safer in our work, and do appear to shut out professionals based on their skin color or native language, then these exams are running *counter* to licensing boards' stated mission of consumer protection, not serving it.

## Should we be using licensing exams at all?

There is no data that correlates licensing exams with safe practice. While exam developers go to tremendous lengths to demonstrate *content validity* of their exams, there have been no studies of psychotherapists that have correlated exam scores or passing with safe or effective practice down the road. What little data does exist about correlates to exam success shows that licensing exam performance aligns closely with GRE scores and academic performance – in other words, that they most directly assess your skill at taking licensing exams.

Even so, there are two kinds of arguments that can be made in favor of the continued use of license exams for the mental health professions. First, the high pass rates on licensing exams can be argued as evidence of their *effectiveness*, not their failure. Examinees meaningfully prepare for the exams, and do, in fact, use the exams to demonstrate key knowledge in the profession. That most people pass their exams doesn't change this fact; if anything, it can indicate that we do a good job preparing new professionals for this key hurdle. Second, it can be argued that even if the exams *aren't* actually valuable in terms of public protection, they still hold value in other ways for the mental health professions. There is some general evidence that licensing exams get more difficult as more people seek to enter the work force of a given profession. While this evidence is debatable (it could also indicate that as more people seek to enter a profession, the proportion of people trying to enter who aren't actually qualified grows), if taken at face value it means that license exams protect the profession from rapid increases in the labor supply, which would drive down salaries as the supply-demand curve changes. Exams also give at least the *appearance* of a high professional standard, even if the reality is a bit more complex.

# The big fixes: Building a better pipeline

There is *absolutely no scientific basis* for the requirements of 60-unit degrees at the master's level, *any* particular unit amount at the doctoral level, or 3,000 supervised hours of experience for licensure. And the scientific basis for licensing exams is highly questionable. Together, these requirements have turned on their head what was supposed to be a careful apprenticeship model that protects the public by ensuring competent care from knowledgeable professionals. What we have instead is a system that rewards wealth and endurance above merit, does not meaningfully improve effectiveness, and shuts out many of those who would otherwise be well-qualified to serve their communities – particularly men and women of color.

The current process of bringing new therapists into the psychotherapy fields is broken. As we seek to build a better professional pipeline, our decisions should be based on scientific evidence where it is available. Included in that science must be a careful evaluation of the true level of need for psychotherapy services.

**What we have instead is a system that rewards wealth and endurance above merit, does not meaningfully improve effectiveness, and shuts out many of those who would otherwise be well-qualified to serve their communities – particularly men and women of color.**

While some may find it morally distasteful, I have no problem with professions raising and lowering their training requirements in response to the ebb and flow of public demand for their services. A profession that is entirely non-responsive to public demands will either produce too many practitioners or too few, and will fail in its exchange of professional standards for public trust. When a profession produces too many practitioners, it makes their services so cheap that the profession wouldn't be worth entering. This was the struggle of the law profession through much of the early

2000s – there were so many newly minted graduates that many could not find adequate employment. Many turned to other professions, and some law schools closed.

When a profession produces too *few* practitioners, the cost of services can become so high and their availability so low that para-professionals and quasi-professionals would seek to meet any demand for them instead, risking public safety. Consider what happens when abortion providers become so scarce that women resort to unlicensed practitioners. Demand for abortion doesn't change much based on the available supply of abortion doctors, but the safety of the abortions women receive certainly does.

It is, of course, debatable where the therapy profession stands in terms of public demand. On one hand, public reports often bemoan the lack of available mental health providers in rural areas and for specific language groups.[107] On the other hand, many therapists will begrudge the difficulty in finding paid positions upon graduation, or achieving adequate income upon licensure. Graduate programs are sometimes blamed for having low admissions standards and flooding the marketplace with underqualified clinicians.

The market forces related to demand for psychotherapy services are complex. This makes determinations about an appropriate number of therapists in any given area – and, by extension, the appropriate level of training needed for entry into mental health – incredibly challenging. Adding what we know about clinical effectiveness, and how quickly it comes, to the mix only makes it more difficult to determine where the professional bar for entry should be.

But what should be clear is that raising or lowering the bar for entry into the psychotherapy professions should not be something that is done at purely a financial level. Raising the cost of therapy training when there appear to be too many therapists would likely have its intended effect: there will be fewer incoming therapists. But these incoming therapists will not be any better than the ones cut out of the mix. Indeed, those left behind by financial constraints may be more likely to be non-white and non-English speaking, the very kinds of therapists we need to be pushing *toward* the field and not away from it.

## Education

None of the psychotherapy professions has gotten demonstrably more effective in the past 30 years. Remember from the beginning of this book that this is a good thing – *30 years ago, psychotherapy was already tremendously effective.* The fact that we haven't gotten markedly better isn't so much evidence of weakness as it is evidence of long-standing strength. This lack of improvement also isn't unique to psychotherapy; recent criticisms of psychotropic medication have also pointed to a lack of improved outcomes in many years.[108]

It is important, though, to consider our lack of improvement in effectiveness as we examine graduate school curricula and the overall educational requirements to become a therapist. If the transition at the master's level from 36-unit to 60-unit degrees has placed hundreds of millions of dollars of student debt on the backs of new therapists and their families, without meaningfully improving the safety or effectiveness of our work, are those expanded requirements truly necessary? Were they worth it?

I'm not sure that my response would be an unequivocal "no" – as I said at the beginning of this book, there are no mustache-twirling villains here. Those who have pushed for higher standards of education in the mental health professions have done so from well-meaning places and in response to important changes in how we think and work. They also have been responding to marketplace forces including competition from other professions and increasing demands from employers. But it is time that we take a hard look at every individual curriculum requirement in mental health, and demand that it be either:

1. scientifically justified as fundamentally necessary to client care;
2. acknowledged as necessary or helpful to some client care, some of the time, and made elective for students; or
3. removed.

Perhaps the most ripe area for curriculum content to be made elective rather than required is in the many courses students today must take on theoretical models of psychotherapy. As I'll discuss later, the "common factors" crowd deserves a victory lap; they have more than adequately demonstrated that a therapist doesn't need to know *every* theory of therapy or even *many* of them to work effectively, and that indeed, the particular theoretical model a therapist chooses has little impact on clinical outcome. So why, then, do programs spend multiple semesters teaching students dozens of models of therapy, most of which the students will never use?

Education can be much more efficient when focused on the core skills of psychotherapy that cut across multiple models. While even most common factors proponents agree that therapists do need to be working from *some* kind of model of therapy, today's students are needlessly over-educated in models that will likely never be relevant to their work, and they aren't given the ability to opt out.

## Supervised experience

Many of us who have gone through the supervision rite of passage can speak eloquently of career-changing experiences with good supervisors, ones who pushed us to become better as therapists or to think about cases differently. An unfortunate few can also speak of career-changing experiences in a negative direction. To be sure, it is at least *possible* that supervision can have a dramatic effect on the quality of a therapist's work.

But how much training do you actually need to be effective? Not very much.

You may have heard of the "10,000-hour rule," popularized by Malcolm Gladwell in his book *Outliers*. In the book, he synthesizes research from a variety of fields and comes to the conclusion that very few people reach top levels of performance with fewer than 10,000 hours of practice.

As it relates to therapy, as well as a variety of other skills, this is a bit of an oversimplification. Scott Miller has taken a closer look at the research Gladwell reviewed, as well as the larger body of literature on the development of performance ability in both therapy and other activities, and came to a more complex and interesting conclusion: Yes, those who reach the *pinnacle* of performance tend to take about 10,000 hours or 10 years to do so. But practice, in and of itself, is a painfully slow road to improved skills. In fact, left to our own devices, skill development in a wide variety of complex tasks generally plateaus after *about 50 hours* of practice.[109] Once we reach a level of performance we consider to be functionally adequate, we don't tend to get a lot better. In therapy, it takes our *confidence* much more time to catch up with our effectiveness, but remember all the studies cited at the beginning of this chapter. They consistently show therapists in their second year of experience to be just as effective as seasoned professionals.

# Skill development in a wide variety of complex tasks generally plateaus after about 50 hours of practice.

To put that into perspective, most master's-level therapists are re-quired to get at several times that much experience *before they even complete their graduate degrees*. It is therefore likely that a great many therapists don't improve at all between graduation and licensure. Their con-fidence may improve, but their actual outcomes – which, remember, *are already really good* – may not.

Moreover, the things we typically do in therapy supervision – those things we think *might* be what make new professionals as effective as sea-soned professionals, and that we think make therapists better as they prepare to go out on their own – actually do very little to improve performance. Case presentations and group discussions, which are the heart and soul of many supervision groups, simply don't appear to make you a better therapist in any measurable way.[110] At least not according to existing research.

So what *does* actually improve therapy outcomes? There are, in fact, meaningful differences in therapist outcomes – all else being equal, some therapists consistently achieve outcomes better than their peers.[111] Those therapists are not necessarily the ones with more experience or even a good supervisor; they are the ones who engage in what Miller and others have called *deliberate practice*, which I briefly mentioned a few pages back. Consider a guitar player as an example: If they learn a song and play it over and over, they'll eventually reach a plateau in terms of their ability to play the song well. They can get better slowly (if at all) by continuing to play the song again and again. But if they want to get better faster, and develop skills that can transfer to other songs, they need to focus specifically on those parts that they *don't* do well.

Miller also addresses the uncomfortable truth that one way of im-proving therapy outcomes overall is by focusing less on those therapies that may work better or worse than others, and focusing instead on those *thera-pists* who are producing poor results. We'll return to that issue in Task 4. For now it will suffice to say that Miller has a strong argument.

## Early efforts at change

The APA has changed their model licensure law, from which states base their individual licensing requirements, to completely remove the requirement for a post-doctoral internship. At first, this seems like precisely the kind of change that's needed, one that perhaps is in keeping with research on clinical effectiveness and client safety. APA's stated rationale for the change, though, doesn't go as far as it could. Their argument for removing the post-doctoral internship has instead been that "graduate students in clinical, counseling, and school psychology receive an average of 1800 to 2000 hours of supervised clinical experience prior to entering the [predoctoral] internship year," where they will do another 1,500 supervised hours.[112] In other words, *they're getting 3,000 total hours of experience anyway.*

It's an understandable rationale, and a reasonable enough one for getting rid of the postdoctoral internship requirement. Unfortunately, it fails to address the bigger issue, which is that there is no evidence that 3,000 hours of supervised experience is either necessary or helpful when compared with other amounts.

In California, where the requirements for family therapists are notoriously and needlessly complex, the state licensing board is developing legislation that would simplify the process for both LMFTs and LPCs. While this is not the same as actually breaching the 3,000-hour total requirement, the changes California is considering would have the practical impact of easing the pathway to licensure, and reducing how long it takes the average practitioner to get through the process.[113]

Other professions have also begun to critically examine whether their training requirements are actually serving the profession and the public appropriately. The American Bar Association has been wrestling with the question of whether law school can be shortened to two years, and medical schools are now hoping to address the crisis of their *under*production of doctors through shortened training programs. The best part of these examinations of training requirements is that they have not been focused just on the raw numbers of practitioners in the field; instead, much of the debate in law and medicine about how much training is needed has focused on serving the public by providing competent service.

You do not need two years of supervised full-time experience to become a competent therapist. Research is abundantly clear on this. Some therapists become as competent as they ever will be in their careers after just 150 hours or so of supervised sessions. Others will not be as effective as their peers no matter how long they are supervised. We should accept this research as it currently stands and adopt training requirements that are sensible, reachable, and truly in keeping with public service.

### Exams

We also should adopt educational and licensure standards that reflect *demonstrated competence*. As I mentioned earlier in this chapter, the likelihood that someone who wants to become a therapist will be able to do so should be based primarily on merit, not money. This might at first sound difficult, given the problems with license exams I've outlined above. But it doesn't have to be; there are a lot of ways to demonstrate merit separate from multiple-choice exams. Universities can adopt entrance exams that assess a prospective student's basic skills as they would likely be developed at the bachelor's level; a student at that point wouldn't be expected to be an expert in issues like suicide assessment, but they should be able to demonstrate basic abilities like relationship-building with new clients that we know are fundamental to treatment outcomes. Practicum and internship sites can adopt completion requirements based on demonstrated skill, ideally through the measurement of client outcomes rather than more subjective measures like supervisor evaluations. I'll discuss such requirements in greater detail in Task 4.

Since licensing exams are unlikely to go away, they should be more directly tied to the knowledge and skills most clearly necessary for safe practice. In other words, a multiple-choice license exam is done best when it is specifically about content like legal and ethical requirements and crisis intervention, and when it allows enough time for even non-native English speakers to fully consider and complete their exams. It is unrealistic and inappropriate to draw further inferences about therapists' safety and skill levels in actually doing therapy based on a multiple-choice exam.

# Is it still worth it?

I'll admit, the data in this chapter is probably the most discouraging of any of the data in this book. We're training new therapists in things that aren't relevant to their success in therapy, requiring them to do apprenticeship that takes far longer than research suggests it needs to, and then putting them through a license exam process that has little to no demonstrable impact on public safety. These barriers make it hard to become a therapist if you aren't independently wealthy, and the financial barriers to entry in the field get worse by the year. They limit the diversity of the psychotherapy professions at a time when the United States population is becoming more diverse, and the professions need to become more diverse to catch up. Every part of our training and apprenticeship model is broken.

And yet, I will argue quite forcefully to those considering getting into the field that it is absolutely worth it to do so. There are clients who need your help. The field is ridiculously expensive to get into, but also rewarding in far more ways than money (and you can certainly make a great living as a therapist, though it is by no means guaranteed).

If you choose to become a therapist, you're likely taking more of a financial gamble than I did. Our incomes haven't kept pace with the climbing cost of entry into the profession. But the good that can be done remains substantial. The rewards you can experience as a psychotherapist go far, far beyond money (and they do *include* money). And the problems that exist in the profession are ones that you can have a direct hand in fixing.

# Taking it personally: What you can do

It may seem at first that these problems are bigger than any individual therapist. One person is not going to change educational standards or the licensing exam process, nor can one of us individually change the larger economic forces that are making it harder to earn a living as a therapist. There are, however, several things you can do to protect yourself from those forces, and to push the field toward change.

### 1. Let money be an explicit factor in decision-making

Therapists are often reluctant to talk with one another about our financial concerns. Perhaps it is out of a sense that as helping professionals, we should somehow be above having money as a motivating factor. But we all have bills to pay, and we do ourselves and each other a disservice by keeping quiet about financial issues in psychotherapy.

If you are considering becoming a therapist, financial considerations apply very directly to your choice of graduate program. As of 2013, stated tuition costs for master's degree programs in psychotherapy in California varied from less than $15,000 to more than $70,000.[114] It's unfortunately quite difficult to know how much your graduate education will *actually* cost, given the difference between a program's stated tuition rate and what students actually pay after financial aid is taken into account (known as the "discount rate").[115] Concerns about cost may be heightened if you are considering attending professional schools or other private institutions, which often charge far more than public institutions while also offering less aid for students. However, pushed in part by new rules from the government and accreditors, programs are slowly becoming more transparent about how much students actually pay, how likely they are to complete their degrees, and how often they are able to find employment once they graduate.

If you are at the internship stage, it's fine to take an unpaid internship if you have the financial means to do so and want to support the cause of the organization where you want to work. But if you are not in those circumstances, taking an unpaid internship that you cannot afford is a recipe for resentment. It's hard to be fully present with clients when there's a constant voice in the back of your head saying "I could be making more money working at Starbucks."

If you're at an unpaid internship in a for-profit setting (particularly after completing your degree), there is a good chance that your internship is actually against the law. Get familiar with the law, consult an employment law attorney, and demand that your employer treat – and pay – you as an employee. Internships in for-profit settings, where owners and investors profit by exploiting early-career therapists, only persist because interns have failed to stand up and challenge the status quo.

If you are licensed, perhaps the most direct step you can take to acknowledge the role of finances in decision-making is to ask for a raise. If you're in private practice, raise your fee. (If you serve on insurance panels, ask them to raise your reimbursement rates.) Admittedly, you may not get the raise you ask for, and local market forces may discourage you from raising your fee by very much. But even in the asking, you will be making a clear statement that your work has value that too often goes unrecognized, and that deserves to be financially rewarded.

## 2. Fight for those behind you

The people who express the most concern about how long and ex-pensive graduate training is tend to be graduate students. Those who have the most to say about difficulties in the internship stage are, as you might guess, interns. And those who are most active in voicing their frustrations about the exam process are those about to go through it.

This is a natural and understandable tendency. After all, we talk about what we know best, and we know best what's happening to us *right now*. Get past the graduate degree stage, and there is a new set of problems for you to attend to. Get past the licensing exam stage, and your focus turns to building your practice or otherwise advancing in your career. We quickly lose interest in making these processes easier for those who follow us. Some of us even fight against changes that would make life easier for new profes-sionals, out of a sense that we would be cheated by such changes – if it was so hard for me to make it through, why make it easier for others?

Researchers call this the "drawbridge effect," and it happens across disciplines. It is easy to fall into the mistaken assumption that those follow-ing you into the profession are dealing with the same type and degree of struggle that you dealt with, and that because you had to fight the way you did to get to where you are now, new professionals should be required to do at least as much, and perhaps more.

While it is psychologically understandable, the drawbridge effect does not serve the mental health professions well. It only keeps those more seasoned professionals, who may have worked their way into positions of influence, from doing anything about the problems that face less experi-enced therapists. But wherever you are in your career path, you can use the experience and influence you have gained so far to help those behind you, and you will likely find it very rewarding to do so. If you are a graduate stu-dent in the second year of your program, you have earned the power and influence to organize a student group to help acclimate first-year students – who will become friends, colleagues, and referral sources for you. If you are an intern, you can share your journey with students to help them navigate the process of finding an internship. You also can provide feedback to your graduate program on what it did well to prepare you for your job, and what it could do better – feedback that accreditors are increasingly requiring pro-grams to gather and use.

One easy way to fight for those behind you is through how you make referrals. Stop referring to clinics that do not pay their interns, and tell those clinics the reason why you have made that choice. (Of course, this assumes that you can meet clients' referral needs without resorting to clinics that don't pay their interns.) Whether you refer clients there or not, if you know of clinics or other settings that should be paying their therapists but aren't, say so publicly. Announce your disapproval of their labor practices at professional gatherings and in any other context you see fit to do so. Some places can be convinced to pay their interns appropriately. Others may need to be embarrassed into doing so.[116]

## 3. Supervise

One of the greatest struggles many pre-licensed therapists experience is in finding quality supervision. Some of this is a raw numbers issue, as new therapists in remote areas – some of whom have completed their academic training online – struggle to find any supervisors at all who are willing to take them on. And some of it is a quality issue, with supervisees hoping to get more from their supervision experience than simple monitoring.

There is an obvious tension here between this and the first suggestion for what you can do about therapist training: Let money be an explicit factor in decision-making. Supervision often doesn't pay well. But therapists who are experienced enough to be able to supervise, and knowledgeable enough to do it well, are often better off financially than their less-experienced or less-successful peers. If you are in a position in your career and financial life where you can dedicate even an hour or two each week to supervising new professionals, you can have a tremendous impact. For new therapists who are near you, one potential solution to today's problems with therapist training is you.

# Task 3:
# Embrace science

Scientific study has a great deal to offer therapy. Recall from the Introduction that meta-analytic studies support our work as extremely effective in general. Cost-effectiveness studies show that treatment typically pays for itself. And specific outcome studies support a wide variety of therapeutic approaches. Though it has its share of weaknesses, the scientific method has dramatically improved our understanding of how mental illness works and how treatment can best be designed.

Still, many therapists would prefer we take a non-scientific approach to our work. Some even push for a dramatic shift in mental health work *away* from science, arguing that it is a fundamentally artistic, indefinable, or even spiritual endeavor.[117]

Perhaps you are one such therapist. Perhaps you rely on intuition and relational awareness to determine how to work with a particular client, and consider therapy to be much more of an art form than a scientific practice. It would be inaccurate to call what you do *guessing*; your interventions are based in experience, even if you can't necessarily explain *why* you're doing a particular thing in that specific way with that specific client. But it also would be inaccurate to say that you are engaging in purposeful treatment planning. You are *being* treatment, rather than *doing* treatment.

There is a rational basis for this approach. The meta-analytic literature consistently shows that the relationship between client and therapist is by far the strongest predictor of therapy outcomes, and that the therapy model used represents, at best, a sliver of that which is ultimately responsible for treatment success.[118] Sure, any sliver is still meaningful, and it is appropriate to try to maximize the effectiveness of our treatments, but these meta-analytic findings suggest that we should actually be emphasizing therapist *ways of being* in the graduate training process much more than we presently do, and *ways of doing* much less than we do today.

Even that change in training emphasis, however, would still be a response to scientific findings. For some, that is exactly the wrong place to look for guidance on how to treat those who are suffering. Scientific inquiry, by its very nature, suggests that the questions being investigated have answers that are objectively true. A more artistic perspective, which is in line with existential and postmodern models of therapy, suggests a pluralistic approach where reality and knowledge are inherently subjective.[119] In this line of thinking, healing can occur more readily by knowing the patient and being in relationship with them than by diagnosing them and applying a scientifically-based treatment.

So are we a scientific field or a non-scientific one? This isn't really an either-or question; any human service profession should involve elements of both. Being over-reliant on science would reduce us to treatment-manual-reciting robots, while being under-reliant on science would keep us from advancing our knowledge about how mental and emotional problems progress and how change commonly happens. But what we are often (and rightly) perceived to be right now is the worst mix of the two: A field that takes on the mantle of science when it serves us, but all too readily disregards science when it becomes even mildly inconvenient.

# We want the mantle of being a scientific field

One of the stated missions of the APA is to "increase recognition of psychology as a science." They describe it simply as the "science of behavior," and advocate for psychology to achieve increased prominence as a STEM (science, technology, engineering, and math) discipline.[120] More than the other therapy professions, psychology training emphasizes science and research.

While the master's-level psychotherapy professions are less explicit in defining their work as scientific (for example, the American Counseling Association does not use the words "science" or "research" anywhere in its mission or in its definition of counseling),[121] all of the psychotherapy professions require their members to practice based on the best available scientific evidence. Here's how they each put this requirement:[122]

**APA Code of Ethics, Standard 2.04:** "Psychologists' work is based upon established scientific and professional knowledge of the discipline."

**ACA Code of Ethics, Introduction to Section C:** "Counselors have a responsibility to the public to engage in counseling practices that are based on rigorous research methodologies."

**AAMFT policy statement:** "AAMFT expects its members to practice based on the best research and clinical evidence available."

**NASW Code of Ethics, Standard 4.01(c):** "Social workers should base practice on recognized knowledge, including empirically based knowledge, relevant to social work and social work ethics."

Clearly, each of the professions expects its members to practice in accordance with scientific knowledge. In advocating for professionals to have job opportunities, the organizations regularly cite the scientific basis for this work. If they said "we mostly just do what we feel is right at the time," they know they would be laughed out of whatever room they happened to be in.

Individual therapists also enjoy the status that comes with being part of a scientific field. Take a room full of therapists and tell them that you oppose how the public and physicians too often see medication as a quick fix for depression, and you can win some easy applause. Anti-depressants are highly overprescribed given the scientific support for their effectiveness, most therapists will likely agree. Physicians and patients alike should attend to the robust research supporting (1) lifestyle changes, including changes in eating, sleeping, and exercise patterns, as a robust first line of response to depression; and (2) psychotherapy, of course, either on its own or in conjunction with medication. Is it so unreasonable, we ask, for doctors to understand the science behind depression treatment and to refer for therapy accordingly?

Turn that same lens on therapists, however, and you'll get a very different response. Is it so unreasonable for therapists to understand the science behind depression treatment and refer for medication accordingly? Many therapists would offer, at best, a hedged answer here. Sure, we might say, science is important, but science only gives us averages and generalities. If we want to most effectively treat the specific person in front of us right now, we need to be able to custom-fit the treatment plan, to invent individual diagnoses, to throw science out the window.

Consider what we're saying there. Physicians and patients should attend to science, but not us. We're somehow immune from needing to understand current science or subject our own work to scientific scrutiny. Is there any other field of health care where you would be comfortable with your health care professional actively discounting what studies show about their work?

Physicians and patients alike should not be blamed for their skepticism of therapy. We're saying that *they* need to really know things, but that it's enough for us to go on instinct. The anti-science sentiment in our field has led to disastrous new "diagnoses" and other examples of therapists falling victim to the mental illness flavor of the week. Each time this happens, it tends to be followed by a correction – which is good. But that correction only calls further attention to the problem we created or bought into in the first place, and gives doubters more ammunition to attack psychotherapy in general as baseless, and psychotherapists as irresponsible. A few examples:

## Diagnosis of troubled children

Nearly 20% of high school boys in the US have received a diagnosis of attention deficit hyperactivity disorder (ADHD), well above traditional estimates that ADHD occurs in 3 to 7 percent of children. Even proponents of broad diagnostic criteria for ADHD are now arguing that it is given too easily.[123] While there are some children who do truly suffer from the disorder, the effects of such rampant diagnosis are only beginning to be understood. Medications for ADHD, which are typically stimulants, have become drugs of choice for many high school and college-age students seeking to improve their school performance.[124] Adults who were diagnosed in childhood with ADHD and put on stimulants may be more prone to other forms of drug abuse in adolescence and adulthood.[125]

Given the reach of American psychology and international pharmaceutical companies, ADHD is primed to rapidly grow in frequency around the developed world.[126] This growth, of course, is not in the raw number of children actually exhibiting attention problems, but rather in the diagnosis and treatment of these problems as an illness requiring expensive (often pharmaceutical) treatment.

In the US, there is a growing perception that the market for ADHD diagnoses, and the drugs that treat them, is saturated. Clinicians are pushing back against the frequency of ADHD diagnoses, and parents, teachers, and clinicians alike appear to be increasingly acknowledging that the diagnosis is treated with skepticism – a significant problem for those who truly do suffer with severe attention problems. But the correction in this case appears not to have been a more general move away from diagnosing children with mental illness. Instead, a different diagnosis has become fashionable.

Diagnoses of childhood bipolar disorder increased more than 4,000% in less than 10 years. That's not a typo – compared with 1994-1995, the diagnosis was given *more than 40 times as often* in 2002-2003. More than half of those diagnosed with childhood bipolar disorder are *also* diagnosed with ADHD,[127] suggesting that the parents of troubled and misbehaving children continue to hold hope that the right diagnosis and the right medication will be the answer. One significant concern in both ADHD and childhood bipolar treatment is that these disorders are increasingly treated with powerful antipsychotic medications despite the fact that these medications are not considered appropriate for behavioral problems.[128]

Psychotherapists and physicians alike have expressed skepticism that so many childhood bipolar cases had simply been lurking undetected until now. There was meaningful pushback against this updated attempt at medicalizing troubled behavior in children. Unfortunately, the correction in the field may be worse than the original problem. Like ADHD before it, childhood bipolar disorder is being replaced by a new diagnostic flavor of the week, this one potentially even more damaging.

Today, there is a movement toward diagnosing personality disorders – diagnoses that are presumed to be long-lasting and essentially incurable – in children exhibiting serious behavior problems.[129] We can only hope that as this trend grows, examples rapidly emerge of children diagnosed with "personality disorders" who, either through treatment or removal from their difficult circumstances, no longer qualify for the diagnosis. While many of these children certainly do have emotional and behavioral difficulties, it is hard to see a clear benefit of applying such a severe diagnosis so early in life.

These diagnoses are often cited as examples of the trouble with the DSM generally, or even with the current state of mental health care as a whole. The lack of biological testing for these disorders (the diagnoses are given solely based on behavioral evidence) leaves professionals reliant on parents' and teachers' reporting of children's behavior. These reports may be influenced by parents' and teachers' stress levels, and thus not truly accurate. Therapists and physicians may be diagnosing for the purpose of giving parents and teachers an explanation for a child's troubled behavior, or to help the child access additional services, rather than on the basis of a truly objective evaluation. (There is, of course, the always-present whiff of self-interest when a therapist offers a diagnosis that *just happens* to be the very thing they specialize in treating. But so many ADHD and childhood bipolar diagnoses are being given by general-practice physicians that it appears unlikely that the increases in these diagnoses are driven primarily by provider self-interest.)

Many therapists do rightly decry the rapid growth in diagnosis and drug treatment of children. Often we see ourselves as the heroes in this fight, offering explanations for a troubled child's behavior that are more adaptive and transient in nature, and providing treatment options that do not involve medication or its side effects. Our own perception, however, does not necessarily line up with that of the public. Surveys show that a large majority of the public does not understand the difference between psychology and psychiatry,[130] and thus may see psychotherapists as complicit in the problem or even as active supporters of it.

Today's waves of fad diagnoses of children may be marginally better than the "satanic ritual abuse" diagnostic fad of the 1980s and 1990s, but to the public, they only reinforce the notion that psychotherapy is no more scientific than exorcism.[131] Ultimately, the public sees – quite accurately – a lack of scientific validity or reliability behind how both doctors and therapists assess, diagnose, and treat troubled children. Where good science exists on the treatment of childhood behavioral problems, many of us aren't following it, and where it doesn't exist, we're allowing the reckless application of questionable diagnostic labels that can impact children for years.

## Substance abuse treatment

The treatment of drug and alcohol abuse in the US is a big industry, with a market value of about $35 billion each year.[132] Much of that goes toward psychotherapy. And much of that psychotherapy is based on a belief set that science does not support.

Drug and alcohol abuse treatment in the US is dominated by 12-step approaches. These approaches are based on the 12 steps of Alcoholics Anonymous, a treatment that was developed some 80 years ago. While many have undoubtedly been helped by 12-step programs, current evidence suggests that this represents only a small sliver of all those who have tried such programs – the overwhelming majority of whom are *not* helped.[133]

Proponents of 12-step programs are quick to defend their work, arguing that substance abuse is notoriously difficult to treat, and that many drug and alcohol abusers need multiple rounds of treatment before one finally works. While that is accurate, research on substance abuse treatment has come a long way in the past 80 years. It now appears likely that, on average, 12-step approaches are actually *worse than doing nothing* when it comes to helping the average drug or alcohol abuser quit. In one of the most comprehensive analyses of various alcohol abuse treatments, AA ranked 37th out of 48 treatment methods. It was well behind the most effective methods, which were brief interventions, motivational enhancement, and GABA agonist medication, but *also* well behind even such minimal interventions as case management (12th), acupuncture (17th), exercise (20th), and the no-intervention-at-all method, simply labeled self-monitoring (30th).[134]

The weaknesses of the treatment industry have been brought to light in a number of recent ways, including the books *The Sober Truth: Debunking the Bad Science Behind 12-Step Programs and the Rehab Industry* and *Inside Rehab* and the documentary movie *The Business of Recovery*.[135] Yet there appears to be very little movement toward scientifically-supported approaches within the industry itself. A proposed 2014 California law to create licensure for substance abuse counselors would have *required* them to use only abstinence-based approaches like AA, even though approaches focused on moderating use and other harm reduction principles appear to be more effective.[136]

The Affordable Care Act is improving access to substance abuse treatment for some 60 million Americans, roughly half of whom had no prior coverage at all for such treatment. The other half had less coverage than what the ACA mandates.[137] Unless those therapists providing substance abuse treatment push for implementation of approaches known to be more effective than the 12 steps, much of the money spent on the new ACA coverage will be wasted.

## Understanding and treating schizophrenia

You may recall from Task 1 that the roots of my particular field – marriage and family therapy – can be traced back to schizophrenia treatment in the 1950s. A number of therapists and researchers noticed that patients diagnosed with schizophrenia were more likely to be quickly reinstitutionalized when they had been released to their families than they were when they had been released to live on their own. While this may have been partly related to individual patients' levels of functioning (the extra family support would be more necessary for those less able to function on their own), the hypothesis quickly developed that family functioning and family interactions worsened the symptoms of schizophrenia. Soon enough, some were hypothesizing that family interactions actually *caused* schizophrenia.

Given the gender-based assumptions of the time, the idea that family interactions could cause schizophrenia directed attention toward mothers, who were presumed to be responsible for child and family functioning. Psychatrist Frieda Fromm-Reichmann coined the term "schizophrenogenic mother" to describe a mother who was at once needy and rejecting, placing her child in what some family therapists labeled a "double-bind." When a child receives conflicting messages that each include some kind of threat, and the child lacks the ability to safely comment on or leave the situation, the theory of the double-bind proposed that acting crazy becomes the only logical solution.

It should be noted family therapists were by no means the only ones pushing this idea. It appeared widely in psychology and psychiatry journals of the time.[138] But family therapists were particularly strong proponents, and it is not a part of our professional history that we are particularly proud of. The notion of the schizophrenogenic mother didn't lose support until the 1970s. Even today, the field of family therapy struggles to escape the long shadow of this mother-blaming stance.

Unfortunately, this was neither the first nor the last example of mental health professionals coalescing around a conventional wisdom of schizophrenia treatment that had a very limited scientific base. The excellent *Mad in America* details how we in the US appear to have actually gone *backwards* in schizophrenia outcomes since the 1970s, as deinstitutionalization largely failed and community-based treatment has been supplanted by jails as a common place for those with schizophrenia to receive long-term care.[139] It tends to be a polarizing book, which you may love or hate depending on your level of belief in the lasting benefits of the antipsychotic medications so widely used today. But it makes a compelling argument that the scientific basis for antipsychotic medications is not much stronger than that which existed for the notion of the schizophrenogenic mother, which itself was not much stronger than the basis for the lobotomies so cruelly and casually practiced a century ago.

::

In each of these instances, there is at least a kernel of truth. Attention deficit disorder and childhood bipolar disorder have almost certainly been overdiagnosed, but there are thousands of children who legitimately qualify for the diagnoses. Many thousands of people have been helped by AA, which was a pioneering treatment at the time of its development; other programs based on the 12 steps are even today the only kind of treatment many can afford for drug problems and other issues that 12-step groups address. And while we can say definitively that mothering does not cause schizophrenia, there is evidence that family dynamics can worsen schizophrenia symptoms while family education can help.[140]

In each case, however, psychotherapists have been quick to jump into nonscientific trends, to jump on a bandwagon that was headed in the wrong direction. And we have been slow to jump off of these bandwagons even when science showed with great clarity the mistakes we were making.

# Don't know much 'bout psychology

Popular wisdom about psychology often contradicts well-established scientific knowledge in the field. Psychology students are prone to believing such myths as:

- The expression of pent-up anger will reduce it
- Full moons increase the frequency of strange behavior
- On a multiple-choice test, a test-taker should stick with their original answer even when it seems like another answer is correct[141]

Even licensed professionals often hold misconceptions directly related to our work. And there is some evidence that psychotherapists today actually hold *less* knowledge about our work than we did a generation ago.

Several years ago I led a study that examined just how much marriage and family therapists actually knew about marriage. Therapists responded to 21 questions about marriage and divorce that had been effectively and conclusively answered in the scientific literature, saying whether they thought each statement was true or false, or whether they didn't know. (Some statements were true, others were myths.) On average, the therapists surveyed got less than half of them right.

Most interesting were the correlations between demographics and responses on individual items.[142] For example, one item was "Married people consider their sex lives more satisfying than single people consider theirs to be." That statement is true; the common *myth* is that single people have more satisfying sex lives. Who was most likely to get that item right? *Therapists who were married themselves.* Another was "Men reap far greater benefits from marriage than women" (that one's factually false; men get greater health benefits from marriage and women greater economic benefits, but both sexes live happier, longer, richer lives when married, on average). Men were more likely to get that right.

There are a couple of ways to think about this. One is that the MFTs in this study had their general knowledge reinforced by their personal experience – that they already knew the fact at issue, and were more confident in that knowledge after they had experienced it themselves. Another, less generous way of thinking about it is that the therapists surveyed *didn't have general knowledge.* If their personal experience didn't tell them whether an item on the survey was true, they either didn't know, or just guessed.

Many therapists will likely wonder here, "So what?" If therapists are using their personal experience rather than the best scientific knowledge currently available, is there any great harm? Science has its flaws as a way of knowing, as we will discuss in more detail. In many cases, what we think we know from science today will be deemed wrong 10 years from now. Can't therapists rely on their own experience instead?

To answer that question, consider this scenario:

*You are a therapist meeting for the first time with Emma, an 18-year-old girl who is trying to sort out her future. Emma is weighing two options: Go to college at a university 100 miles away, or go to work in her smaller but more familiar hometown. While Emma is interested in building a career, it is a higher priority to her that she ultimately find a husband and get married. She says she's not interested in going to college if it will make it harder for her to have a family.*

The therapist could simply stay neutral on this question and provide company for the client as she sorts this out for herself. As we discussed in Task 1, however, that seems to be an abdication of the therapist's responsibility to actively facilitate positive change. So let's assume here that the therapist wants to provide information that will be of value to the client.

Let's also assume that, of course, the therapist is going to be sensitive to the unique individual circumstances of this case. Scientific research usually offers averages and general conclusions, not clear indications of what will be best for a specific individual at a specific time. No study provides a client-specific crystal ball.

All that said, what is *most likely* to be in the client's best interests here? The answer is very clearly that she should go to college. Not only will that support her dream of building a career, but she *also* is statistically more likely to get married – and a lot less likely to get divorced – if she's a college graduate.[143] A therapist who is ignorant of this fact might, based on the therapist's own experience or even their best guess, hold a belief that college education runs counter to the likelihood that a woman will get married. That therapist would be flat wrong, and would risk giving Emma guidance that would actively hinder her chances at achieving *either one* of her dreams.

Or consider a more pernicious example. Is a woman at greater risk of violence if she is single or if she is married? One of the critiques of the institution of marriage has been that it facilitates intimate partner violence by providing a structure where violence will be discounted by police and courts.[144] Some therapists, adopting this critique, might imply or outright tell clients that they should avoid getting married.

They're wrong.

Major national studies in the US, Canada, and Australia, involving tens of thousands of participants and accounting for the under-reporting of intimate partner violence, have concluded that the risk of becoming a victim of violence is *three to four times greater* for unmarried women than for married women.[145] Of course, this is a correlation, not a cause-effect relationship. Married people are less likely to engage in drug use and a wide variety of other behavior that increases the risk of becoming a victim of violence. But a therapist who suggests to female clients that they are safer as unmarried women – something *more than two-thirds of therapists* in my study incorrectly believed – is offering bad advice.

It hasn't always been this way. Some 16 years before my dissertation, a group of family life educators was surveyed on their knowledge of many of the same issues. They didn't get all of them right. But they got a large majority.[146]

There is good reason to believe that if we paid more attention to science, our clients would experience better outcomes. We may perceive that our felt sense of a client, combined with our knowledge of their unique circumstances, positions us well to anticipate what kind of intervention will be needed and what the results will be. But many studies have shown that therapists perform consistently *worse* than actuarial tables at predicting client outcomes. Those tables base their predictions on a small number of variables and, by design, do *not* account for clinical judgment of the unique circumstances of each case.[147] More than 50 years ago, psychologist Paul Meehl argued passionately against therapists' stubborn insistence on using clinical judgment to make predictions when statistical methods known to be more accurate were available. He called it "foolish, and I would even say immoral."[148]

What has happened within the mental health fields that we continue to resist the benefits of an increasingly useful and sophisticated knowledge base for our work? There appear to be two sets of reasons. The first has to do with the inherent weaknesses of scientific study, while the second is more philosophical in nature: Therapists are questioning science itself as a meaningful way of knowing.

# Bad science

In early 2015, a team of German researchers made headlines around the world when their clinical trial showed that eating dark chocolate could actually *help* weight loss when combined with a low-carbohydrate diet. *Shape* magazine, London's *Daily Star*, and Prevention.com were just a few of the hundreds of media outlets that ran stories announcing dark chocolate's newfound virtue without any critical examination of the research.

The study was real. It was just intentionally bad.

Lead author John Bohannon and his team wanted to show just how easy it was for poorly designed research to make headlines. (Earlier, Bohannon had demonstrated with a laughably poor research paper just how easy it was to get published in open-access journals that claim to have meaningful peer review processes.) They studied just 15 people, and assessed them on 18 variables. This is a recipe for "false positives," finding relationships in the sample that are purely random and not actually due to the thing being tested. And that was the idea: Bohannon and his colleagues wanted to demonstrate just how easy it was to gain "scientific" support for even the most ludicrous hypothesis.

A bit of a statistics primer may be helpful here. (If you're familiar with alpha and $p$ as used in research, feel free to skip ahead to "There are two major problems...") In order to draw a large conclusion from any study, we have to be reasonably sure that any relationship between two variables that we see in our data isn't just random noise. Flip a coin four times, and you're most likely to get two heads and two tails, but you also could get four heads just by chance. If that happened, you wouldn't want to go running around town saying you've got a magic always-heads coin. Other people would try to duplicate your trick, and would eventually figure out that you just have an ordinary coin. You would look foolish, and those who tried to replicate your finding would rightly grumble about how you wasted everyone's time.

No true scientist wants that kind of reputation. Non-replicable studies are a huge problem in the research world, with one recent estimate suggesting that more than half of all laboratory research could not be replicated, costing $28 billion a year.[149] And that estimate comes from life sciences, generally considered "hard science" because of its focus on laboratory work, relative to the "soft science" of psychology. Psychology and psychiatry fared the worst among all scientific categories in one analysis of how much published findings skew toward positive results.[150]

But because we do research with a limited number of participants – a sample – there's no way to know with absolute certainty that what we see in our sample would show up in the larger population as a whole. A wide variety of statistical tests can produce a $p$ value, which is essentially the possibility that what we've found would have occurred by chance if there were actually *no* relationship between variables in the population as a whole. A p value is expressed as a decimal: If our analysis gives a $p$ of 0.03, then there's just a 3% chance that we've found a fluke.

Researchers don't want to be running around making false claims, and reputable journals don't want to publish them. (There has been, as Bohannon pointed out in his earlier study, significant and unfortunate recent growth in the *non*-reputable journal market.) So we have to figure out how much risk we're willing to take that the thing we think we've found is, in actuality, just happening at random. This level of risk for a false positive that we will tolerate is called "alpha," and it is set at the beginning of a study, typically before data is even collected.

In most studies, we set "alpha" at 0.05, meaning that we're not willing to take any more than a 5% chance that a relationship we think we've found is actually just random noise. If the $p$ value we then find is less than the alpha we set at the beginning of our study, we can say that we've found a *statistically significant result*. We know it isn't a *guarantee* that what we've found is a real thing and not just random chance, but there's less than a 5% chance that we got it wrong.

There are two major problems with using alpha and p-values in this way, though. The first is that our risk tolerance, usually 5%, is for *a single test of a single relationship*. Testing 18 variables at once and using a sample of the size Bohannon's team did, even when there is no *actual* relationship between the variables you're testing, the likelihood that at least one test will *appear* to show a meaningful relationship is more than 60%.[151] The researchers in the chocolate study knew they had a great chance that their design would allow them to at least report *something*. Sure enough, they found that those people on a low-carb-plus-chocolate diet lost weight about 10 percent faster than those just on a low-carb diet, and their scores on a well-being survey were a bit better. Both of these differences, while small, reached statistical significance. Lost in the discussion is that each group (treatment, low-carb, low-carb-plus-chocolate) was *just five people*.

This happens all too frequently in behavioral science. In what researchers call *p-hacking*, elements of an experimental design can be changed – sometimes even after data has been collected – to ensure the greatest likelihood that a study will find *something* that qualifies as a significant result. Researchers also sometimes guarantee themselves a positive outcome by "Hypothesizing After Results are Known," a practice so common it has come to be known simply as HARKing. In each case, the positive findings make a study more likely to get published, getting the authors media attention and improved career prospects.

In psychotherapy, studies of various interventions are plagued with precisely the problems that the German researchers exploited so well: Lots of variables combined with low sample sizes are ripe conditions for false positives.

The second problem that comes from using p-values and alpha in this way is that it becomes easy to make a statistically significant finding look more useful than it actually is. Studies with large sample sizes are prone to finding *statistical* significance where there isn't any *practical* significance. Consider a recent study that suggested couples who met online were less likely to get divorced and more likely to be happy in their relationships.[152] Because the study included almost 20,000 participants, it easily reached statistical significance – the researchers could say confidently that they found a real difference between those who met online and those who didn't. But the differences between groups were so small as to be largely inconsequential: 7.7% versus 6% on divorce rate, and 5.48 versus 5.64 on a 7-point scale of happiness. The study offered virtually no predictive value. It might be marginally better for you to meet your spouse online, but other factors unique to you and your spouse could quickly outweigh the online-versus-offline difference. Nonetheless, this study also received major coverage in popular media around the world. The study's effect size, which we discussed back in the Introduction and which is a far more useful statistical measure of the strength of a relationship, was near zero.

These designs are usually not intended to deceive. Studying psychotherapy is no easy or cheap task, as participants must be recruited who are willing to share information on their therapy process over a period of weeks or months. Researchers must spend a significant amount of time gathering data from each participant. And those researchers often are interested in a number of potential outcomes from whatever it is they are studying, so they gather data on a wide variety of variables. It is quite common in the psychotherapy literature to see studies of 10-30 participants assessed on a dozen or more different variables, or to see studies of hundreds of participants that casually ignore the question of whether their results offer any real predictive value.

Researchers report positive results from these studies because they genuinely believe them to be true and meaningful. They typically aren't trying to deceive colleagues or the public. But they are, quite possibly, deceiving themselves. One analysis of psychotherapy studies found that reportedly-significant findings had $p$ values that clustered just barely under 0.05, suggesting that many authors focused their energy on anything they could report as a positive result. Given the overall numbers of variables in many of these studies, it is likely that a meaningful chunk of supposedly significant research results in psychotherapy are flukes. (One prominent researcher has concluded that most published findings – not just in psychology, but *in all fields*, are likely to ultimately be false based on these very statistical concerns.[153]) To be sure, there is ample reason to be skeptical of much of the research base in psychotherapy.

But that isn't reason to disregard science entirely. And it seems many therapists do exactly that, replacing the imperfect scientific way of knowing with other, far less certain ways of knowing. Like personal experience, belief, or just plain guessing.

# Discounting science as a way of knowing

One of the reasons I have heard many therapists give for discounting scientific knowledge is the importance of culture. At first it can appear hard to argue with this. Psychological research published in the US *has* historically over-relied on samples of educated, middle-class white people. It makes sense to question the relevance of such findings for people from other income and education levels, and other racial backgrounds.

Too often lost in that discussion, though, is the fact that researchers have actually come a long way in addressing this problem. There are now, for many individual and family problems, specific interventions that have been rigorously tested with a wide variety of specific racial and religious groups. Assessment instruments often have multiple norming samples to determine whether meaningful differences should be expected based on the client's background. And as the population of therapists continues to become more diverse, our knowledge about things like gender and culture matching in therapy grows as well. In short, if you have a client from a minority culture experiencing a specific mental health issue, there's a good chance that there are relevant studies on specific interventions for that problem with a client from that culture. There's a great deal of work still be done in understanding what forms of treatment, or what adaptations to existing treatments, will work best with specific populations. But the great amount of work that has been done in this area cannot be simply dismissed.

Culture also doesn't suffice as a reason to willfully ignore general knowledge. For one thing, at least some impacts of gender and culture wash away quickly in therapy. Studies of therapist-client matching – that is, pairing a client of a particular race or gender with a therapist who shares that same race or gender – largely show that any impacts of such matches vanish after a few sessions.[154] For another, in the absence of studies of a particular culture, general studies of interventions for a particular problem can at least offer a useful place to start. Furthermore, we may be placing so much emphasis on cultural and contextual factors that we lose the proverbial forest for the trees – again, actuarial tables based on very limited information about people (race and income sometimes being among the factors considered) offer consistently more effective predictions of therapy outcome than therapists' clinical judgment.[155]

Scientific findings in psychotherapy need to be critiqued and contextualized to be useful. In most cases, however, they should not be simply dismissed. They represent an important way of knowing, and ultimately of advancing our field.

Many of today's therapists argue otherwise.

## The rise of postmodernism

Postmodernism is the philosophical backbone of many of today's favored models of psychotherapy. Considered by some to be the "third wave" in psychotherapy (following the "first wave" of psychoanalytic approaches and the "second wave" of behavioral approaches), postmodern models of treatment were largely developed and popularized in the 1980s and 1990s and have continued to be favored models for many therapists since.[156]

Narrative Therapy, Solution-Focused Therapy, Collaborative Language Systems, and others all rely on a shared set of postmodern assumptions, including:

- Human beings are inherently meaning-making
- Meaning, and therefore reality, is socially constructed through the use of language
- Reality is subjective, allowing for multiple truths
- Knowledge is relational, developed through shared investigation[157]

There is, of course, much to like and value here. There are also good reasons why these models came into favor, including their responsiveness to (rightful) criticism that psychotherapy has been historically unresponsive to matters of race, culture, and context. For far too long, members of marginalized populations had an experience of therapy that was unaware at best, and insulting at worst.[158] The positioning of therapist as an expert served only to reinforce middle- to upper-class white ways of being as the supposed "right" ones and other ways of being as wrong or unhealthy. Postmodern approaches do far better at honoring the experiences of *all* clients, and recognizing the limitations of therapists' knowledge.

At the same time, the postmodern philosophy is often understood as running actively opposed to the pursuit of an objective truth that is core to the scientific method. Consider the assumption above that reality is inherently subjective. From this stance, it is argued that scientific research is too clouded by its own assumptions to reach anything that could truly be considered a shared truth; the mere act of posing and researching a scientific question positions the researcher above their subjects. This makes science an act of imposition, not collaboration. Postmodern practitioners, by and large, do not wholly discount *research*, but they often do discount *science*, preferring to focus attention on qualitative (descriptive) studies rather than those that seek objective truth or predictive utility.[159]

This is problematic for the psychotherapy field in multiple ways. Philosophically, postmodernism as its leading proponents understand it does *not* discount science, it merely treats it as one of many ways of knowing.

Postmodernism does not take the stance that *any* way of knowing is inherently invalid, and indeed believes in a pluralistic pursuit of understanding that makes room for averages as well as exceptions.[160] True postmodernism suggests that, like all ways of knowing, science can and should *inform* the social development of consensus around key ideas. They simply do not believe that science should have the sole authority to dictate those ideas.

The second problem this generates is more practical. As described above, scientific knowledge certainly has limitations. However, the qualitative research preferred by postmodernists *also* has key limitations, most notably in its inability to ask or evaluate questions of prediction that could meaningfully improve treatment. Qualitative methods can be used to address the questions, "Did you feel like this treatment worked?" and "What about this treatment did you experience as most helpful?" But it requires quantitative methods to answer questions of whether a treatment actually changed clients' behavior, and whether it did so more or less quickly than another form of treatment. Simply put, an over-reliance on qualitative methods will improve our understanding of the client experience, but will not tell us whether our efforts to use that understanding to improve treatment had any measurable impact.

The two forms of research can co-exist well, with qualitative studies helping inform the questions that should be asked by quantitative researchers and vice versa.[161] This would enable us to advance both our general effectiveness in therapy and our understanding of when generalities will fail us and more culture- or context-specific treatments are preferable.

Such informed advancement, however, seems not to be the desire of some postmodern therapists. Far from offering the kind of true collaboration in treatment that postmodern approaches suggest, which requires *both* parties to bring relevant skills and knowledge to the table, some therapists take calls for a "not-knowing" stance in therapy quite literally – approaching therapy as if they had never received any training, or as if it had no value in the task at hand.[162] This is not what the developers of postmodern models had in mind. Those developers have attempted to differentiate the humility of a "not-knowing" stance from the emptiness of a "know-nothing" stance. Leaders in postmodern therapy have expressed concern about therapists who perceive no responsibility to practice in accordance with science, or to direct treatment in any meaningful way.

This discussion is not, of course, meant to cast aspersions on therapists simply for using postmodern principles or practices, or to devalue postmodernism more generally. The postmodern movement in psychotherapy has given a great deal to clients and to psychotherapy in general, including an awakening to issues of diversity and presumptions of rightness that the field had too long ignored. However, postmodernism in its truest form offers no excuse for ignorance of, or animosity toward, the development and use of scientific knowledge.

## The threat of treatment manuals

Some of the concern about science appears to stem from a "slippery slope" concern about where scientific adherence would lead us. Manualized treatments are loved by researchers because the manuals standardize therapy, making it at least theoretically possible to assess a treatment model even when utilized by different therapists treating different clients in different clinical settings. Those same manualized treatments are often loathed by practitioners, who believe that working from a treatment manual reduces therapists to "technicians," disallowing the use of individual intuition and placing therapeutic technique above relationship.[163]

This concern is well-justified. There are increasing mandates on therapists in public mental health to work from lists of pre-approved therapies. Where I live (Los Angeles), public mental health treatment focused on prevention and early intervention can only be provided from a list of pre-approved, manualized approaches, in which the provider must have specific training.[164] Even therapists who are generally supportive of evidence-based practices in psychotherapy show negative attitudes toward treatment manuals.[165]

However, treatment manuals come in many forms. And while there *are* efforts underfoot to remove the therapist from therapy entirely – efforts that are almost surely doomed to fail – treatment manuals aren't part of those efforts.

While some treatment manuals are much more specific and prescriptive than others, manuals almost universally limit themselves to what they describe as essential elements of their approach – conceptualizations and key interventions that make the treatment distinct from other models. These help a therapist plan and organize therapy, but do not aim to supplant the therapist's skill in *applying* the therapy. In fact, many treatment manuals are explicit about the need for clinicians to be adaptive, to account for cultural and contextual factors, and to use their skills and creativity to bring the key elements of the model to life. Take this example from the treatment manual for emotionally focused therapy:

> "The EFT therapist is active, engaged, and flexible, discovering with his or her clients the possibilities in their relationship. The person of the therapist is an important factor here, but there are also set techniques and interventions. The EFT therapist uses his or her personal style and resources to create a context for techniques and in-interventions, and to connect with each client's experience."[166]

There are some who are experimenting with removing the therapist entirely from the therapy equation. Artificial intelligence is growing increasingly powerful, and is driving the development of a wide variety of tools to simulate the experience of meeting with a therapist or coach.[167] There's surely a great philosophical debate to be had about whether a human being could *ever* relate to a machine in the way that we relate to other humans – territory that's been skillfully mined by movies like *Her* and *Ex Machina*. But for our purposes, it will suffice to say that we are decades and perhaps generations away from even having to worry about the question. As I've hinted at already and will discuss in greater detail shortly, the therapy part of any therapy doesn't appear to be the driving force behind why it works. Indeed, the specific model or techniques used account for just a few percent of the variability in treatment outcomes.

There is scientific consensus that the quality of the relationship between therapist and client is far more influential.[168] The development of that relationship – building trust and rapport with a new client, often as they are in a difficult and vulnerable emotional state – is something that, while perhaps not *indisputably* human, is far ahead of the capabilities of current artificial intelligence. It also is largely what makes manualized treatments work.

# Falling behind

Therapists' tendency to disavow scientific knowledge as valid or valuable is unfortunate on multiple levels. Not only does it leave us less able to inform clients of what treatments will likely work best for them at a given time, but it also harms our standing with the public. Therapists are widely regarded as "tender minded" and unscientific in our work – untrustworthy and not worth the high fees we charge, precisely because we lack a scientific perspective.[169]

We as professionals also often actively ignore neuropsychological research that can provide the strongest evidence in history supporting the benefits of psychotherapy. Here is just a sampling:[170]

- The act of labeling emotions appears to increase activation of the prefrontal cortex, thereby regulating emotional activation in the amygdala. (Journaling, a homework assignment often given in therapy, appears to have similar effects.)
- The construction of new narratives in therapy facilitates neural network integration in the brain. Changing perspectives builds connections between the dorsal-lateral regions and the orbital-medial areas of the prefrontal cortex. This integration "creates resilience to stress and a hedge against resorting to dissociation, as well as greater affect tolerance and ego strength."[171]
- Therapy helps clients achieve a balance between emotional activation in the amygdala and declarative or conscious processing in the hippocampus and prefrontal cortex.

This is very much the tip of the iceberg – researchers' understanding of neurobiology now offers overwhelming support for psychotherapy, not just in confirming that it works but in explaining *how and why* it works. Notably, the research is most powerful in supporting the work of some of the therapists who are least interested in it; Cozolino talks in great depth about the physiological changes in the brain that appear to come with the construction of new narratives, which, while certainly accomplished across many types of psychotherapy, is the central point of narrative therapy.

---

**Researchers' understanding of neurobiology now offers overwhelming support for psychotherapy, not just in confirming that it works but in explaining *how and why* it works.**

---

Think about what this means for psychotherapy's standing in the health care world. With solid evidence of effectiveness and explanations for that effectiveness based in hard science, psychotherapy can now stand toe-to-toe with other interventions, and we *should* often win. Yet most therapists have very little awareness of even the most basic of brain functions, and as we've discussed above, show no great interest in using science to support their – our – work.

Our willful ignorance of science, and even active resistance to it, has led other fields to address the problems we should be addressing, slowly eating away at public perception that therapists are necessary at all. As one example, consider the following description of the science of behavioral economics:

"It is a systematic means of describing how people make decisions and how they change their minds; how they choose someone to love and marry, someone perhaps to hate and even kill; whether, coming upon a pile of money, they will steal from it, leave it alone, or even add to it; why they may fear one thing and yearn for something only slightly different; why they'll punish one sort of behavior while rewarding a similar one."[172]

Isn't that psychology?

Behavioral economists have crunched large behavioral data sets into fascinating findings about human behavior using economic analysis. They have found, for example, that the death penalty has little to no deterrent effect on crime. They have also found that *who a child's parents are* matters a lot more than *what those parents do* during parenting when it comes to improving their child's school achievement.[173]

The work of behavioral economists clearly has tremendous value. There is also clear overlap with the processes that psychologists and other psychotherapists can and should be investigating.

Behavioral economics is a fascinating science, but most behavioral economists are more interested in change *events* than in change *processes*. And changes in functioning that will be truly long-standing tend to happen in processes. If we therapists truly believe that relationships such as that between client and therapist are transformative, we need to be able to make that case in a manner that is as compelling and well-informed as the cases made by behavioral economists and by pharmaceutical companies.

We can do it. Our argument – that the therapeutic relationship is transformative, and that this transformation does not happen in a single event – is actually far better than those made by behavioral economists and even by the drug companies when it comes to facilitating long-term change. But we need to know what that case is and how to talk about it. And to do that, we must get past our resistance to science.

Acknowledging that good science supports our work, and that we as a field should be responsible for practicing in accordance with scientific findings, doesn't reduce us to automatons. In fact, understanding and promoting the science of neurological change in the brain would make it very clear to both therapists and the public just how important the *relationship* part of a therapeutic relationship really is.

# The big fixes

Some of the calls for psychotherapy to be more science-based have sometimes been frustratingly non-specific about how we can get there. They also have sometimes not accounted for all the good and useful pieces of postmodernism that we would not want to leave behind in a movement toward science-based practice.

### Simple scientifically-supported interventions

The value of science in supporting an individual therapist's work might be best illustrated with this example: You have a new client who is experiencing struggles in her marriage and symptoms of depression. According to multiple studies, there is *one question* you can ask her that, if you use her answer as the basis of treatment, will meaningfully improve the chance of treatment success. Any guess as to what that question is?

This particular combination of presenting problems is quite common. While both men and women are prone to experience depression and marital distress together, it seems to be especially common among women. If you know what to ask women in this situation, your treatment outcomes with them can improve.[174]

The question to ask your new client is simple: *Which came first?* If the depression came before the marital struggles, then treating the depression through a combination of medication (if needed) and individual therapy can ease the marital problems. Depression takes a toll on a marriage! Her spouse would surely be relieved to see the depression ease. On the other hand, if the marital problems came first, the couple should be referred to couple therapy. As the relationship improves, so too should the client's mood. Being in a bad relationship is depressing!

This particular finding may seem trivial at first. But there are two reasons why it is critically important that therapists possess scientific knowledge of these kinds of treatment issues. First, *it makes us better at what we do*. Far too many therapists presented with this combination of problems would default to whatever form of therapy they believe is indicated, without asking (or worse, with active disregard for) the key question of which problem came first. In this instance, treating the wrong thing is not only not helpful, it can be actively harmful: Treating depression in a woman whose marital problems actually came first is likely to put further strain on the marriage, and the depression treatment is much more likely to fail. If the depression came first, treating the marital problems that result from depression without effectively treating the cause of those problems similarly offers little.

Secondly, awareness of and responsiveness to scientific knowledge like this *helps us talk to the public and other professionals*. Bear in mind that most people suffering from symptoms of depression do not first seek treatment from a therapist. They go to their family physician.[175] Both on an individual level and as a profession overall, therapists need to be able to go to physicians and say something to the effect of, "You'll see this in your office a lot. This one simple question can help you know when to refer for therapy and when to treat with medication. Your outcomes will improve."

This is only one example of a simple, scientifically-supported intervention that could be applied by therapists from all theoretical perspectives. Others abound in the literature. Consider our earlier discussion of substance abuse treatment, where motivational enhancement and brief interventions represented the most effective treatments available; given their low cost and strong support, it should generally be these processes, and not 12-step programs, that are our first-line referrals for substance abuse. Training programs, from the graduate level through continuing education, would do well to highlight these kinds of findings. (To be fair, many already do.) And the ultimate responsibility falls upon us as individual therapists to remain current in the literature such that we are providing the most effective treatment possible, an issue I'll return to when discussing what you specifically can do.

## Harnessing non-specific effects

At the end of the day, what matters most about a treatment isn't how well it lines up against other treatments, but how well its overall impact lines up against its risks. A placebo effect is, after all, still an effect. Whether a treatment works is a determination based on the *combination* of specific effects (those attributable to a treatment itself) and nonspecific effects (those that come with a treatment, like expectancy and placebo effects, but not actually due to the treatment itself)

In an excellent comparison of studies on depression, Harald Walach and Irving Kirsch weighed the literature on antidepressants with the literature on herbal remedies. Noting the substantial side effects associated with many antidepressant medications, including the sexual side effects experienced by roughly three in four people taking SSRIs, Wallach and Kirsch concluded, "Rather than being a front-line treatment, [antidepressants] should typically be used as a last resort."

What should be the *first* resort, then? It's easy and self-serving for therapists to say "therapy, of course," but here Wallach and Kirsch are at their most impressive. If expectancy is a key driver of effectiveness in treating depression, they argue, we should have the best results if we provide whatever treatment will maximize this expectancy.

"Providing a good explanatory myth and preparing a convincing therapeutic ritual are among the common factors of all therapies. Hence we can hypothesize that for many people, the potential for nonspecific effects is greater in complementary and alternative treatments. This is particularly true of people who have a worldview compatible with the application of "natural" products and who have a belief system favoring complementary and alternative treatments. For others, who subscribe to a more rational and mechanistic approach to diseases, conventional medical treatments may be more effective, although the risks with which they are associated might preclude their use. For still others, psychotherapy might provide the greatest expectancy effects, and thereby the greatest therapeutic benefit. [...] Regardless of treatment type, *nonspecific effects can be better harnessed in believers.*"[176] (emphasis mine)

In other words, if a client believes a treatment will work, it is more likely to work. Drug companies have actually been *so* effective in teaching the public that drugs can solve their problems that they have created a bit of a monster. In recent years, the effectiveness of placebo pills – pills with no actual drug in them – has been rapidly increasing. One study of a proposed new medication for schizophrenia was halted when participants in the placebo group responded *twice as well* as researchers had expected.[177] For mild to moderate depression, a meta-analysis of recent studies found placebo to work just as well as antidepressant medication.[178]

Meanwhile, the expectancy effects of therapy may be on the decline. A meta-analysis of depression studies over the past 40 years has shown cognitive-behavioral therapy, while still quite effective, to be growing less effective over time. Because the model itself has changed very little, researchers speculated that the shift was due to decreased expectancy.[179] Indeed, skepticism that therapy will work remains a top reason why people do not seek it out, behind only access issues like cost and lack of coverage.[180]

There is a powerful expectation of improvement and convenience that comes with taking a pill. That expectation is not always present when someone comes to therapy. Taking a pill has risks, but can *feel* much less dangerous than therapy because therapists usually ask clients to be open about their fears and vulnerabilities. Therapy works, but it also *is* work. It isn't easy for most clients. Given the power of expectancy, clients may be more willing to engage in a therapeutic process if they have an expectation at the beginning that it will be effective for them. So how can we offer that expectation? Our own personal experiences and beliefs are often not enough.

*We need science.*

We need to know, and be able to knowledgably discuss, the decades of literature showing how effective we are in general. We need the more specific research of today showing how different modalities of therapy can effectively treat a wide variety of emotional struggles. We need to be able to explain why we have chosen to work the way we do. We need to be able to offer something more than "I believe it will work for you, so you should too." Offering such proclamations without supporting evidence makes us no different from psychics or snake oil salesmen.

And we can't sell clients on the effectiveness of therapy using science while simultaneously arguing that science should have no influence on our work. We can't have it both ways.

---

We can't sell clients on the effectiveness of therapy using science while simultaneously arguing that science should have no influence on our work. We can't have it both ways.

---

### Big data

One of the most promising avenues of research in psychotherapy is in the use of massive data sets. The electronic storage, retrieval, and analysis of data is far less expensive today than it was even a decade ago, and as computing power continues to increase, it is becoming possible to conduct highly sophisticated analyses of thousands or even millions of health records at once. This kind of analysis is already being used to determine whether differences exist between professions in how effectively we treat various disorders. These studies barely scratch the surface of what future researchers may be able to do.

At first this may sound like a championing of behavioral economics. While that field does fascinate me, remember that behavioral economists are largely interested in change events, rather than change processes. What I'm talking about is a brand new opportunity to bring analytic power to bear on the process of therapy for thousands of clients rather than the dozens commonly used in today's research samples. Imagine a study where 100,000 hours of client sessions are transcribed and analyzed in a fully-automated process that records not just spoken words but tone-of-voice measures, talk-turn lengths, pupil dilation, facial expression, and more. This analysis could define pivotal change events in therapy that today go unrecognized. It could finally help us identify those factors that make some therapists better than others, as we discussed briefly in Task 2 and will address further in the next chapter. And this analysis could be done in a matter of minutes.

We're not there yet, but we will get there in my lifetime. Health care in general is moving to electronic health records, and those records are becoming increasingly standardized, making it easier to do large-scale analyses of them. Videorecording of sessions is becoming easier and cheaper with each new generation of digital devices, and the growth of online therapy suggests that the commonality of such recordings – easy to do when you and the client are both already on camera – will only continue to increase.[181]

Not every therapist will be eager to participate in such large-scale studies or to adjust their practices based on what these studies find. Those of us who ignore the approaching tide of big-data research in psychotherapy do so at our own peril, however. As we will see in Task 4, greater accountability for therapists, including accountability to scientifically-based standards of care, is an inevitability. It is being forced upon us, whether we like it or not. And it is *only* through science that we will be able to continue to justify our professional status and high fees.

# Taking it personally: What you can do

If your graduate degree program did not include a great deal of science, or if your degree is a bit dated, all is not lost. You can develop your scientific literacy at any career stage. The "scientist-practitioner gap" that many in the field have complained about for decades is easily resolvable when clinicians take on a curious stance toward scientific knowledge. That stance can and should even be selfish: Approaching scientific literature with an attitude of "What can you do for me and my clients?" can yield surprising and highly useful results. Here are three techniques to help orient your practice within a strong scientific base.

## 1. Be a skeptic, not a cynic

Using science as a way of knowing can prevent us from offering bad advice or ineffective therapy to clients in need. There is clearly good reason for skepticism of scientific findings, given the weaknesses in many of the studies in our field – especially those most likely to make headlines. But if we discard *all* science based on the weaknesses in *some* science, we lose any ability to claim the mantle of being a scientific field. The loss of respectability that would come with such a choice would be sad, but fully predictable and arguably even deserved.

Good skepticism takes practice. It requires an ability to differentiate good science from bad. It requires understanding that "good" and "bad" here are relative terms, as even the best studies have some weaknesses. It requires knowing that *statistical* significance is not the same thing as clinical or practical significance. Smaller sample sizes should mean bigger doubts about whether a study's findings can be replicated, while larger sample sizes raise the risk that researchers are touting a statistically significant finding that has little real-world value. Even when studies report strong effect sizes, we need to be wary of how the researchers organized their studies. Selection bias, response bias, and a wide range of other problems may still be present. Still, a well-done study can have *tremendous* real-world value, impacting the way we think and work.

Cynicism is easy. You don't need to know anything about the scientific process to discount the overall value of research. Much like the non-advice-giving stance discussed in Task 1, cynicism toward research serves as a very effective way for therapists to abdicate our responsibility to know and work from a shared knowledge base, to keep current with a changing field, or to have some reasonable basis for the interventions we choose. But cynicism toward research also keeps us mired in outdated and discredited ideas about mental health and treatment, and makes us look like laggards in the world of health care.

Media outlets generally cannot be trusted to serve as effective filters of scientific research. While some science writers for major media outlets are in fact very knowledgeable about the research process (I'm particularly fond of Tara Parker-Pope, who writes at The Well blog for the *New York Times*), media outlets will often happily publish weak research if it comes with an attention-grabbing headline. They exist to build readership and sell advertising to that readership, so getting attention is often more important than getting the science right.

There are, however, more trustworthy sources available when it comes to the science of psychotherapy. Peer-reviewed journals published by professional associations are usually safe sources. And a number of books about therapy have gone to great lengths to not just understand the science supporting our work, but to report it in a way that is compelling to the reader. My top recommendations for your bookshelf (each of which is, as of this writing, on its second edition):

- *The Heart and Soul of Change: Delivering what works in therapy*, by Barry Duncan, Scott Miller, Bruce Wampold, & Mark Hubble
- *The Neuroscience of Psychotherapy: Healing the social brain*, by Louis Cozolino

- *The Developing Mind: How relationships and the brain interact to shape who we are*, by Daniel Siegel

Each of these books describes, using understandable language, strong research findings that fundamentally support the work of therapy as a healing interpersonal relationship. Together they make an incredibly strong case for psychotherapy as a front-line treatment for a wide variety of problematic behaviors. Each step you take to understand these arguments and share them with others outside the therapy room is a step toward psychotherapy being regarded as a solidly scientific field.

## 2. Be an evidence-based therapist

Many therapists lament the move in public mental health settings toward a vision of "evidence-based practice" that amounts to working only from an approved list of therapies. It's a gross distortion of the term, but it's one that many agencies and decision-makers have seen as necessary in light of therapists' resistance to conducting treatment in a way that is reasonably defensible. At any given time in treatment, we need to be able to inform our clients of where we are in the therapy process, what particular treatment or intervention we are in the middle of, and why we're doing it that way. These are necessary elements of informed consent for therapy, and ones that many therapists in practice would struggle with.

Our resistance to working from checklists and therapy scripts is understandable; such tools devalue our training and experience in favor of someone else's idea of what effective therapy should look like. I'm in quite strong agreement that we should not be so restricted, and the research agrees with us – consider the many studies cited earlier in this book that show that the particular method of treatment is much less important to therapy outcome than the relationship between client and therapist.

But we also have a responsibility to know what we're doing and be able to defend our treatment choices at any given time. There is no good argument for resistance there. The way to fight back against the forces of standardization and over-manualization of treatment is with evidence-based treatment (using the term more properly). Here is how the term is better defined:

"[T]he term 'evidence-based' is not the same as 'empirically based' or 'empirically validated' which usually refer to specific therapy models that are based on and supported by research data. Instead, EBP refers to the process of *using* empirical data to make decisions about how to best care for one's clients."[182]

In other words, true evidence-based treatment allows for a fair amount of flexibility in therapy as long as we can explain and defend *why* we are using the form of treatment we've chosen. Treatment planning that is truly evidence-based will lead to more thoughtful, intentional, and effective care, and rather than being constrictive, you should find it opening avenues of treatment you may not have previously considered.

Evidence-based practice involves thoughtfully balancing multiple types of information:[183]

- **Client and extratherapeutic factors.** Much of what determines success in therapy is not based on the therapy itself. Client readiness and motivation for treatment have a big impact. The client may express a preference for a particular kind of therapy or therapist; meeting these preferences seems likely to harness the non-specific effects discussed a few pages back, increasing the likelihood that the client will benefit from treatment by increasing their expectation that they will benefit. The client's identity, including gender, race, nationality, disability, sexual orientation, and other factors can also be considered here. The simple fact that a treatment is known to work with one population does not mean it should automatically be presumed to work with all populations. Once therapy has begun, clients have varying levels of social support and additional resources they can draw on to help the therapy process succeed. That these factors are beyond the reach of the therapist does not mean they should be ignored; clients with strong support systems and relatively mild problems may not need treatment at all.[184]
- **Research evidence.** Part of why I am so fond of this multipronged conceptualization of evidence-based practice is that it acknowledges and even advocates for consideration of research as *one of* several factors that combine to inform a treatment decision. Research ideally informs us rather than taking over for us. This stance allows you to plumb the rich depths of profes-

sional books and journals for guidance *and* to put their findings in the proper context when other factors suggest doing something different. Research evidence can be used at the beginning of treatment to choose whether to work with a particular client or refer out; it also can serve as a useful reference point throughout therapy for selecting specific therapeutic techniques.

- **Relational factors.** Speaking of research, it consistently shows that one of the strongest contributors to a successful outcome in therapy is the allegiance between therapist and client. This appears to be true regardless of the therapist's theoretical orientation; models like cognitive-behavior therapy that may be perceived among practitioners as colder are just as dependent on a strong therapist-client relationship as other models. This is not a simple case of clients liking or being grateful for therapy when it works. The relationship developed *at the beginning of therapy* is predictive of outcome. And therapists can do well to adjust treatment based on feedback clients give specifically in regard to the therapist-client relationship as the client experiences it.[185]

- **Therapist factors.** In Task 2, we talked a lot about the therapist factors that *don't* appear to influence outcome – like level of experience. There are, however, therapist factors that are important to consider because they *can* impact therapy outcome. Most important is therapist competency, an issue we will cover in detail in the next chapter; some therapists are measurably better than others, and there are specific steps you can take to become more competent. Suffice to say that if you are aware of a potentially-useful form of treatment for a given client but lack training in it, that lack of training could lead to underconfident and unskilled delivery of the treatment, hurting outcomes. Better to work from a model that you know well and feel comfortable using. Therapist biases about a wide variety of issues, including client race, gender, income, and even weight, have also been shown to have a meaningful impact on treatment outcome,[186] showing the importance of not just knowing your own biases but actively working to counter them in supervision or in your own therapy.

Evidence-based practice involves the consideration of *all of these* areas in the development and continual refining of a defensible treatment plan. We don't all have to agree – and indeed, we shouldn't all agree – on how to best treat a specific client, as we each have different beliefs, different training, and different skills. For any given client, a number of different treatment plans could be successfully defended. But there needs to be *some* basis for the treatment decisions we make.

Using these factors can prevent a lot of therapeutic mistakes, from treating clients unlikely to succeed with us to over-emphasizing techniques at the expense of the therapeutic relationship. If you've not done it before, it can be an interesting exercise to see how well you can defend your current treatment plans based on your knowledge of how the factors listed here apply in each case. Once you're able to succinctly state the basis for your treatment plans, you can approach treatment secure and confident that your work would stand up to even critical outside scrutiny.

### 3. Use a map

While we have many, many models for doing psychotherapy, they tend to do the same things, just using different vocabulary and mildly different points of emphasis. This is the conclusion of common factors researchers, who have made a convincing case in the past 20 years that our field's emphasis on designing a better way of doing therapy – building a better mousetrap, so to speak – has been largely a waste. Many studies seeming to show that one model of therapy is better than others for treating a particular disorder are authored by the model developers themselves, often using themselves as the study's therapists. They then mislabel the positive impacts of their enthusiasm for and belief in the model as positive impacts of the model itself.

Common factors scholars have pulled no punches in their critique of how we train for and perform therapy. They forcefully argue that few, if any, models of therapy have been shown to be more effective than other models for therapy. Even if some models did work better than others, the impact of model on treatment outcome would be just a sliver – far less than the impact of client factors like motivation for treatment, and far less than the impact of the relationship between client and therapist.

Even strong adherents to the common factors argument, though, still say you need a model to do therapy. For one thing, the notion that *any* approach is just as good as any other (or no approach at all) is "a silly position since it puts an impressive empirically validated model like emotionally focused therapy (Johnson, 1996) on the same level as tarot cards, palm reading, and Ouija boards."[187] Rather, common factors adherents argue that *among effective therapies* there are little overall differences in the outcome of treatment. So a common factors argument should not be used as a reason to discount models of therapy overall, or to work without an accepted model for treatment.

Remember the taxi metaphor from earlier in this book? Models of therapy can be thought of like maps to help the taxi driver get from pickup point to destination. The driver might use a road map to get where they're going – that would make good sense. But they also could use a topographic (elevation) map, a traffic map, a trail map (off-roading!), or a map that combines these. It may indeed not matter which map the driver chooses. As long as they have *a map of some kind*, they can tell the passenger at any time where they are, where they've been, how they got there, and what's coming next. The driver can also reasonably estimate how far it is to the destination.

Now consider instead a driver who uses no map at all. At the start of the drive, driving south seems like a good idea, so they do that. After a while, it seems a good time to go west, so the driver turns right. Feeling a bit lost and a bit anxious, another right turn is made, this one at a sharper angle. And then the taxi is simply back where it started. Absent any map at all, the driver can't assure the passenger that therapy is headed in the right direction, as the driver can't really know for sure themselves. They wander. They may come back to the same place several times. If they get to the destination, it is through some combination of a felt sense of how to get there, and pure luck. This is the plight of the "eclectic" (or, more recently fashionable, "integrative") therapist.

Like taxi drivers, therapists over time learn their territory well. We find shortcuts that work reliably well for us. We learn how to navigate rough traffic or normal weather patterns at different times of day and different times of year. Neither I nor the common factors folks would argue that the map should take precedence over the territory, so to speak. But simply working from a model does not preclude individual creativity or personality in the delivery of that model, nor should it. A map is a guide, not a prison. It can help you more confidently explain where you are, where you've been, and where you're going next at any point in the therapy process. It should be limiting only insofar as it discourages you from going the wrong way.

# Task 4:
# Become accountable

The research we reviewed in Task 3 is clear: The model that a therapist uses typically has little to no impact on treatment outcome. While it is important that therapists be working from *some* kind of model, those that are generally accepted in the field appear to have similar effectiveness for most problems.

Left out of that discussion, however, is the impact of the therapist. There is a dirty little secret in training programs, at clinics, and around our profession: Some therapists are better than others.

---

## There is a dirty little secret around our profession: Some therapists are better than others.

---

Several studies have shown this, but one of the larger and more recent studies to clearly demonstrate this fact was mentioned back in Task 1. I'll call it "the Okiishi study" as shorthand here. In a study of more than 5,000 clients seeing more than 70 therapists at a university counseling clinic, a wide variety of factors including therapist gender, experience level, theoretical model, and training type (counseling psychology, clinical psychology, social work, or marriage and family therapy) had *no* link to therapeutic outcome. But there *were* meaningful differences among individual therapists. While the clients of even the worst therapists improved, those working with the best therapists saw almost *three times* as much benefit, and got there in fewer average sessions (Table 1).

Several other studies have come to similar conclusions. For reasons we do not fully understand, some therapists achieve consistently better outcomes than their colleagues. The reasons for this do not appear to be related to therapist age, gender, or ethnicity; theoretical model; level of experience; or type of training.

This finding raises some ethical and moral questions. Consider the following:

- Should therapists whose outcomes are consistently higher than their peers get paid more – and those whose outcomes are low be paid less?

*Table 1. Average client improvement and average number of sessions, comparing best and worst therapists*

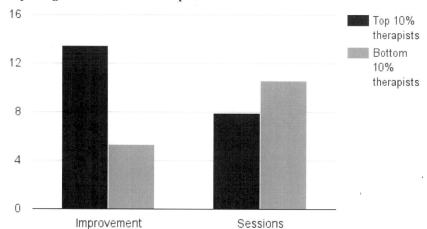

*Source data: Okiishi et al., 2006.[188]*

- Should clinics where therapists have large caseloads gather and use – perhaps even share or publish – improvement data for each therapist on staff?
- Should those therapists who consistently have worse results than their colleagues be required to attend additional training, or even risk being fired?

Remember that in the Okiishi study, even the clients of the least effective therapists experienced meaningful improvement on average. This might lead you to a more permissive stance, encouraging therapists whose outcomes are worse to address the difference as best they can, but wanting to avoid any actions these therapists might experience as punitive. Their clients *are* getting better, after all.

However, there was a subset of clients in that study, just as in any large clinic, who actually got worse as they went through treatment. The worst therapists had *twice as many* clients deteriorate compared to the best therapists (10.6% versus 5.2%). If you are working with clients with severe struggles, where deterioration may mean hospitalization, this perhaps gives added urgency to the evaluation and, where needed, retraining or even dismissal of therapists whose work is not as effective as that of others.

As we will see, fear of punishment is one of several reasons why therapists are reluctant to engage in any kind of meaningful individual evaluation of their work. However, our lack of courage in this area serves to protect the least effective therapists, holding back the overall effectiveness of psychotherapy and preventing a great deal of possible good.

Because the Okiishi study focused on one clinic, its authors knew immediately that the data they had gathered could be applied in such a way that would improve client care. One earlier study showed that a surgical patient's risk of death could be three times higher just as a result of choosing the wrong hospital. Another showed that life expectancy after a diagnosis of cystic fibrosis expanded from 5 years to 20 years as a result of providers and treatment centers having the courage to make their death rates public. So Okiishi's team knew their data, if used properly, would have real impact. They developed a number of specific recommendations for how the individual data gathered from their study could be used to benefit all of the therapists and clients at that clinic:

- The clinic could assign more clients to the most effective therapists.
- The clinic could make outcome information available to clients to use in selecting a therapist.
- The clinic could retrain, more closely observe, or even potentially reassign therapists with exceptionally high deterioration rates.

Each of these seemed likely to have a positive impact on the overall outcomes of the clinic. And none of them could be implemented, because before the study was even started, the researchers agreed with the therapists to keep the identities of individual therapists private. The best the researchers could do was to provide each therapist with a statistical report showing their effectiveness rates, and encourage each therapist to reflect on the report and find ways to improve their work.

Like most therapists, those in this study faced no accountability at all. They could be great or they could be terrible in terms of their outcomes compared with those of their peers, and it wouldn't matter. They all got the same suggestion, one that wasn't specific enough to be especially useful.

# Reasons for resistance

There are good – or at least understandable – reasons for therapists to be concerned about individual accountability. There's the obvious one, that any therapist with even mild insecurity about their work would worry greatly about the possibility that they would be exposed as the proverbial weak link in their clinic or community. There's the fear that supervisors or clients might take greater meaning than is justified from small differences among clinicians in therapy outcomes. There's the fear that they may lose their reputation or even their job over what might be little more than a streak of bad luck in therapy. In any setting where clients are not assigned to therapists at random, therapists may fear that differences in outcome have more to do with who picked them than with the quality of their work.

Some supervisors and administrators also are reluctant to implement data collection about individual therapists that could provide comparative effectiveness information. They may worry that therapists who know such a scheme is in place would pick and choose their clients, working only with those who seem most likely to help their effectiveness numbers. They may worry about fostering an environment of competition, rather than collegiality, among therapists working together at the same site. They may worry about legal liability if the data appears to show one therapist producing worse outcomes than others and they don't take immediate steps to either fix the problem or remove that therapist.

Perhaps most common among both therapists and their bosses is concern about the measurement process itself. Clients come in with a wide variety of problems at vastly different levels of severity. Therapists work in different ways with different constellations of clients (for example, in family treatment, should data be gathered from each family member or just one?). For therapists with smaller caseloads, consider the weaknesses in smaller studies we discussed in Task 3. Even what appears at first to be a large difference between therapists might not be meaningful – it could just be a fluke – if each therapist is only seeing a few clients.

Together, these reasons are often taken as more than sufficient to justify many therapists' decisions to not expose themselves or their employees to meaningful individual accountability. That's unfortunate, as these concerns are resolvable, and the potential for good that could come out of such data is significant.

## Solvable problems

Let's look at each of those fears individually. While I may not be able to do much to proactively resolve any insecurity you may have about your work, I can at least offer reassurance that it is tremendously likely that assessing your practice will make you *more* secure in the quality of the services you provide, not less. In the Okiishi study, even the individual therapist who performed the worst overall still saw improvement in their clients, on average. Only two of the 71 therapists in the study were singled out as having unusually high deterioration rates. You probably don't think you're among the worst 3% of therapists in your clinic or area, but if you do, wouldn't it be a tremendous relief to have data showing that isn't the case? There would be a relatively small risk of being proven right, one which would simply call for actions that you probably should be taking anyway to improve your work. And there would be a high probability of being proven wrong.

Fundamentally, the process of assessing and being accountable for your practice, if done right, is a low-risk, high-reward proposition: If you're doing well, it offers you a concrete measure of that. You can use that data with employers and potentially even to promote your practice to prospective clients. If you're doing less well than you would like, gathering data on your practice can show specifically where you can improve, which is much more useful than simply having a general sense that you could potentially do better. Scott Miller goes so far as to call the initial collection of outcome data a no-risk proposition, since the act of collecting outcome data in and of itself can dramatically improve outcomes. "So no downside exists to determining your baseline effectiveness," Miller writes. "One either is proven effective or becomes more effective in the process."[189]

Many of the remaining concerns can be alleviated through clarity on how accountability data will be used and how it will be interpreted. The concern that clients and supervisors could place greater weight on small individual differences than is appropriate could be addressed in a number of ways. Supervisors can be clear with supervisees that they know small differences are often not meaningful, and can act accordingly. In a large clinic, hospital, or other setting that uses data on individual therapists, those therapists can be grouped by quartile rather than listed in rank order. And of course, much of this concern comes down to a fear of how the data will be used: If a therapist whose clients improved by 11 points on average in the past year gets a bonus, while a therapist whose clients improved by 10.95 points on average in the past year does not, the therapist left out has a justifiable complaint. Such a small difference, even on a year's worth of clients, is probably not statistically significant.

If you've been practicing for a while, you may have had the experience of your success rates going in waves. You'll have a great April, and then a terrible May, and then start to see an upswing again in June. No therapist wants to be punished for a string of bad luck. Perhaps even more to the point, therapists who are struggling with issues in their personal lives and know their clinical work has suffered for it would not want to lose their jobs or careers over a few bad weeks or even bad months, so long as they are maintaining professionalism and doing the best they can with clients. This too is an issue about how data will be used. Consider three possible interpretations of data about a therapist who does not appear to be doing as well as others in the clinic:

- She's had a run of bad luck.
- She's going through a tough time, and needs to focus on maintaining connection with her clients, or consider taking time off.
- She's a bad therapist, or simply not a fit for the field.

The first interpretation is friendly, but not especially useful to either the therapist or the supervisor. There isn't much to do but hope things get better. The last is too severe, and doesn't match the reality of the situation; going through a difficult time in your personal life might mean that you should consider taking time off for the moment, but all therapists experience personal struggles, and these do not indicate that someone is unfit for the field. Like all data, the numbers that are used to make therapists accountable have to be considered in the proper context.

Speaking of context, when clients are not assigned randomly among therapists, then it may very well be inappropriate to compare one therapist with another in the same clinic. If one therapist works with severe depression, while another works with anxiety disorders and a third specializes in substance use disorders, accountability should be more focused on basic questions of client improvement versus baseline than on how much one therapist's clients are improving relative to clients of other therapists.

The concerns of supervisors and administrators are similarly resolvable. They would be right to think that there is an incentive for therapists to pick and choose clients if therapists will be rewarded for having clients with the least symptoms at termination, or if taking tough cases is otherwise disincentivized. The solution is to not disincentivize tough cases. Either have a staffer assigning cases as randomly as possible, or (if a reward scheme is to be used at all) ensure that the reward scheme encourages therapists to take on challenges rather than avoiding them. In any kind of public discussion of outcomes, make it clear that you appreciate those therapists who have taken on the toughest cases coming in to the clinic.

Competition is another key concern of supervisors and administrators weighing whether and how to use client outcome data. Particularly if bonuses or other rewards are given to top performers, therapists who should be working collaboratively may try to undermine each other's work. There are a number of ways to address this concern. An obvious one would be to limit the use of individual data to (confidential) evaluation and training, with any performance bonuses awarded to the entire clinical staff for their aggregate success rates. In this way any one individual therapist's success also becomes a success of the entire group. Another way to resolve this concern would be to take steps to create what Miller labeled a "culture of excellence," where modeling and social pressure form an expectation that staff members will be positive, collaborative, and accountable.[190]

Concerns about legal liability are perhaps most easily dismissed. Supervisors and administrators may worry that the outcome data they gather could be used against them if a client sues over treatment provided by a staff therapist whose outcome numbers had been lagging. However, it seems more likely that such data would be helpful in defending *against* claims of inadequate supervision or monitoring of a therapist's work. The collection of outcome data shows that the therapist's work is being carefully tracked. Training efforts for those therapists whose numbers lag clearly indicate responsible supervision. And in a worst-case scenario where a poorly-performing therapist who is unable to improve needs to be let go, outcome data can serve as a strong justification for such a firing. Courts are unlikely to find supervisor liability in cases where care was appropriately supervised but simply didn't work, and are also unlikely to move unlawful-termination claims forward when there is clear documentation of the employee's performance and failed efforts to improve their work.[191] As accountability in mental health continues to grow, it seems likely that the standard of care will ultimately become the routine gathering and analysis of client outcome data. Twenty years from now, the greater liability risk may be for those supervisors and work settings who do *not* measure client outcomes.

The measurement process itself provokes many of the greatest concerns among clinicians, supervisors, and administrators. We all invest a lot of time, energy, and money into building our careers as therapists, and once we are in jobs we like, the idea that a job could be pulled away from us is threatening – especially if that action is taken based on a flawed measurement process. As discussed in Task 2, one of the most important processes for measuring therapist preparedness – licensing exams – are themselves a deeply flawed and ineffective process, likely keeping well-qualified therapists out while allowing too many bad therapists in, and creating understandable distrust in *any* formal process of evaluating clinicians.

The process of addressing this concern is a bit more involved, but it brings forward some of the best principles of good science. Evaluative questions for clinicians must be asked in a specific and intelligent way that aligns with the mission and purpose of the organization. The evaluative tools need to be appropriate to the evaluation question. The evaluative process should be conducted with a high level of openness and transparency. Results should be considered in context of their limitations. And the entire process should be recursive, where the results of the evaluative process can influence the organization, and the organization takes steps to impact the results (and perhaps the methodology, depending on how well everyone feels it worked) of the next evaluative process.

When an evaluative process is developed in keeping with these principles and in collaboration with those who will be evaluated, not only are therapists often quick to "get on board," many are actively enthusiastic about it. I have been pleasantly surprised at the degree to which the younger therapists with whom I have worked yearn for meaningful and actionable feedback on their performance. In some cases, they spent years in classes where most of the students got A grades – preventing them from being able to assess how they were performing relative to their classmates – and then went on to early clinical experiences where every supervisee was subjectively evaluated by the supervisor as "excellent."

We all want to be doing our jobs well. For most of us, if we aren't succeeding, we desperately want to know that so we can do something about it. There are probably a few of us who would prefer the naïve and known-to-be-wrong belief that all therapists really are excellent – that "average" is somehow the bottom of the scale. But I would venture that there are many, many more who would deeply value more objective measures of their impact on clients' lives, so long as they could trust that those measures were being applied in a manner that was fair and transparent.

# "The dustbin of quackery"

Early in 2012, I was summoned to the office of California State Senator Ted Lieu. The Senator had learned in the prior months about a practice known as *reparative* or *conversion therapy*, where a therapist works to change the client's sexual orientation. Often, these clients are teenagers pushed into therapy by their parents, who do not want to accept that their son or daughter is gay.

There is no scientific evidence that these practices are generally effective, though there are a number of anecdotal reports of clients who found the treatment effective and were grateful to have gone through it. There are also a number of anecdotal reports of clients who have been gravely damaged by the therapy, who believed that there was something wrong or broken in them because of what their therapist had told them, and who went on to consider or attempt suicide after failing out of the treatment.

The one neutral researcher who had published findings that seemed to support reparative therapy rescinded his own findings in 2013, apologizing to the gay and lesbian community for the damage he felt his work had caused. That same year, the American Psychological Association released a report called "Appropriate Therapeutic Responses to Sexual Orientation" that summarized the existing literature on reparative therapies. It discouraged therapists from attempting any therapy with the goal of changing sexual orientation. Several other professional associations for therapists have come to similar conclusions.[192]

Senator Lieu was alarmed to learn that in spite of these recommendations, many therapists in California were still practicing reparative therapy. Indeed, the state seemed to be something of a hotbed of reparative therapy activity, with many key figures in that approach based in the state. He wanted to know whether the associations would support an effort to ban, or at least restrict, the practice. None of the associations said "yes" at that first meeting – with legislation, the devil is often in the details, and the associations all wanted to see specific legal language for such a ban before offering support. But no one said "no" either, and that was enough for Senator Lieu and his staff to move forward.

Following a long and challenging year that advocates spent working the bill through legislative committees and many rounds of changes, in September 2013 Governor Jerry Brown signed Senate Bill 1172 into law. It bans licensed therapists in California from performing reparative therapies with minors, and subjects the therapist to discipline against their license if they do such therapy.

When signing the law, Governor Brown made a forceful statement opposing reparative therapies. He expressed hope that with this new law, such techniques would be "relegated to the dustbin of quackery."

I agree wholeheartedly that reparative or conversion therapies have no place in a legitimate therapist's practice. But that dustbin of quackery? It's pretty empty.

Here, quick: Name one form of talk therapy in mental health that was frequently used in the past, but that we collectively stopped using because it didn't work. Can you name any?

Sure, you can probably name some forms of *medical* practice for mental health problems that we don't use today: Bloodletting, lobotomies, and electroshock therapy are only used in the rarest and most unresponsive of cases. But think specifically in terms of our modern definition of psychotherapy. Can you name a single form of *talk therapy*, going back to the early 1900s, that has been purposefully discarded from the field?

To be sure, there are some models of treatment that have *fallen out of favor* for various reasons. The Encounter Groups and other unconventional therapies of the 1960s and 1970s aren't common any more, but they are still used. Same for the "rebirthing therapies" that earned infamy in the 1990s when some clients died of asphyxiation – they also still exist, just without the role-play of birth that might actually kill you. Like many others, these models of therapy never had much scientific support, and yet they seemed to experience and ebb and flow of popularity where nothing is ever really gotten rid of. Their lack of demonstrated effectiveness has not left them dead, just dormant.

This is one area where psychotherapy is quite different from other areas of professional health care. Lots of forms of health care practice are discarded when they are revealed to be less safe or effective than other methods. But psychotherapists seem uniquely susceptible to the siren song of pseudoscience, with therapists (and, indeed, sometimes clients) latching on tightly to methods that range from dubious to fully debunked, and continuing to practice them for decades beyond their appropriate shelf life.

It might be tempting to chalk this up to laziness or other negative traits on the part of some therapists, but the reality is more complicated.[193] Many therapists do not understand the scientific process that leads us to accept some practices and discard others, as we discussed in Task 3. We are easily swayed by confirmation bias when a client experiences positive change, and we want to think it was the treatment that made the difference rather than anything else in the client's life. And often, we have invested many years and many thousands of dollars to hone our skills in a particular way of working. We are then understandably reluctant to go through the discomfort of letting go of old ways in favor of new ones.

In the case of fringe therapies such as conversion therapy, or innovative therapies and delivery systems, the accountability burden must be higher. It is a logical error to say "many forms of therapy are similarly effective, and this is a form of therapy, therefore it must be as effective as the others." Even the strongest champions of common factors argue against the idea that *any* form of therapy will work with *any* problem. They limit their argument to *accepted* therapies – and even then, they acknowledge that for a few problems there *do* seem to be some treatments that work better than others, such as exposure therapy for specific phobias.

# Almost all ethical violations go unpunished

The Hoffman report, to which I referred in Task 1, demonstrated just how far professional associations can go to protect their members from ethical accountability. Through a combination of vague policy language and minimalist investigation processes (the APA usually conducted what they called "paper investigations" of ethical violations, without ever calling possible witnesses or actively gathering additional information), the APA's ethics branch exercised virtually no meaningful enforcement of the professional standards of behavior it claimed to uphold. In 2011, the APA Ethics Committee reviewed just four cases.[194] They haven't put their annual reports online since.

While the APA has been rightly criticized for this, it is hardly alone in its failure to root out damaging practices in the field. Nor is it alone in exerting so little effort in the area. Professional associations in psychotherapy have largely moved away from ethics *enforcement* and toward ethics *education* for their members – a shift that is wholly consistent with the associations' desire, as discussed in Task 1, to protect themselves and their members above protecting the integrity and advancement of the professions.

The simple fact of the matter is that the overwhelming majority of even serious ethical violations among mental health professionals are never reported. Even of those relative few that *are* reported to a state licensing board or professional ethics committee, only a small minority result in any disciplinary action at all.

You may at first think it would be difficult to estimate how many serious ethical violations occur, or that estimates would rely on debatable assumptions about what behaviors qualify as ethics violations. But given the opportunity via anonymous surveys, many therapists own up to actions that are indisputably outside of accepted professional boundaries.

- One of every five psychologists limits their treatment records to the client's name, the date, and the fee.[195] A small minority say they don't keep any treatment records at all.[196]
- Surveys of psychologists suggest that as many as 1 in 25 will have a sexual relationship with a client at some point in their careers.[197]

When it comes to getting therapists to own up to their own questionable behavior, even anonymous surveys have their pitfalls. The data above may reflect only a portion of the frequency with which these acts occur. One interesting way of assessing the frequency of ethical violations in therapy is to ask therapists how often they have observed their peers making questionable decisions. On average, each therapist appears to be witness to more than one ethical problem each year, with confidentiality issues, boundary issues, and payment issues by far the most commonly observed. This suggests that ethically questionable behaviors (the determination of a violation is up to an ethics committee), while not common, occur with much more regularity than disciplinary statistics would suggest.[198]

Many of these acts are never reported, making it impossible for a licensing board or ethics committee to do anything about them. But even when unethical or unprofessional acts are reported, they may not result in discipline. From July 2013 through June 2014, California's licensing boards for psychologists, LPCs, LCSWs, and LMFTs received a combined total of 1,886 consumer complaints – a low number, considering the boards together govern more than 120,000 licensed and registered mental health professionals.[199] In that same span, the boards issued just 133 final disciplinary orders, many of *those* stemming not from consumer complaints but from criminal convictions of therapists (in many cases, for driving under the influence of alcohol or drugs).[200]

Of course, not every complaint is deserving of discipline. Consumers sometimes complain over treatment that was professionally done but ineffective, dislike of policies that they had actively agreed to in the informed consent process, or other concerns that do not represent unprofessional behavior on the part of the therapist. But it is also likely true that some complaints do represent unprofessional conduct that ultimately goes undisciplined, either for lack of supporting evidence or due to other reasons.

Most psychotherapy occurs in private, in a closed office, between a trained and trusted professional and a client who may be in a vulnerable emotional state. This is why psychotherapy is a profession and not just a job. It is also why a robust enforcement process is necessary for the minority of therapists who misuse the trust placed in them, by ignoring professional standards of behavior.

It is unrealistic to expect that every bad behavior will be caught. But the hands-off approach taken by professional associations suggests a troubling lack of desire to purge corrupt practices from psychotherapy. The more involved disciplinary process among licensing boards retains its more punitive nature, but it is slow – California's board for master's-level therapists routinely takes more than two years to investigate a complaint and determine a punishment[201] – and often ineffective. Together, these hobbled processes for addressing unethical behavior in psychotherapy ensure that the worst of us will remain among us.

Perhaps worse, our collective failure to meaningfully address ethical lapses creates a perception among younger therapists that adherence to ethical standards isn't particularly important. This is not a new problem: Almost 30 years ago, a study of graduate students in psychology found that almost half *would* do less to address the unethical behavior of a colleague than they knew they *should* do, even when the unethical behavior at hand – sex with a client, or exhibiting poor judgment and erratic behavior linked to a drinking problem – represented a major breach.[202]

# Individual and collective accountability

Accountability for keeping up with current standards of practice can be viewed through two lenses: Individual and collective. On a collective level, if any professional group fails to keep up with advances in technology and service delivery, they risk the profession's extinction. Consider travel agents: In the age of booking travel over the Internet, there are very few travel agents left. It isn't that individual travel agents were violating the standards of their field. It was that those standards – reflecting the collective profession – didn't adapt quickly enough to the world around them, and the entire profession was largely left behind.

The psychotherapy professions are arguably falling into a similar place. While our work is tremendously effective, we have been slow to adapt to changes to the world around us, all too often digging in our heels around a structure of therapy that includes clients coming to our offices once a week for a 50-minute therapy hour for an indeterminate amount of time. Our collective accountability – to payors, government agencies, and ultimately, the public – is not terribly strong, and we in many ways can appear to thumb our noses at these groups.

Our individual accountability as professionals is *also* low. On an individual level, there is cause for concern if one violates the standards within their profession. In psychotherapy, that's pretty hard to do. The professional standards (in the form of legal scopes of practice, and ethical guidelines) have been written so broadly that it's often a challenge to establish that any one individual is operating outside of those broad standards. Because therapy happens in private, even when serious legal and ethical violations take place they can be difficult to prove, allowing potentially dangerous therapists to remain in the profession. While supervisors appear to take their gatekeeping role seriously, the reality is that it is nearly impossible to keep a determined student or supervisee – even an incompetent one – out of the profession. Once licensed, those of us in private practice never have to prove on an individual level that what we're doing is current or even that it's working.

Physicians have much higher collective accountability. If medicine isn't working, patients and governments will sue drug and device makers, who have to go through a robust proving process before these products are safe and effective enough to be sold. Notably, physicians take on a high degree of accountability on an *individual* level as well: Medical students receive a wealth of formal and informal evaluation, through their supervisors and multiple standardized exams; surgeons are scored on their outcomes throughout their careers; a number of schemes for evaluating physician efficiency have been proposed and evaluated in connection with changes in Medicare reimbursement.[203]

Recall the metaphor for therapy I used back in Task 1, of getting into a taxi while wearing a blindfold. If you are the passenger, it might soothe you a bit to know that taxis in general are safe, and tend to get to the right place – if they weren't and didn't, the local transportation authority would shut them down. It would likely be even more comforting to know that *this specific driver* has a solid track record. As psychotherapists, we typically don't bother to demonstrate either one.

# The big fixes

In the other tasks I've discussed in this text, many of the big fixes need to come from us. Mental health professionals, acting collectively through our professional associations, can accomplish big things for our field.

This one is different. Most of the big fixes here will *not* come from us. They will come from the outside. They have already begun. And they will be imposed upon us whether we like it or not.

## Revenge of the clients

When you buy a car, you can get a great deal of objective information about it. You can learn its price, of course, but also its horsepower, its mileage per gallon, its performance in crash tests, and on and on. You also can get – indeed, sellers are *required* to inform you of – a great deal of information when buying a household appliance. The "Energy Guide" label will appear on the appliance, telling you in big, bold letters how much energy that particular model uses, how that stacks up against similar models, and how much you can expect to pay over the course of a year for the energy needed to run it.

You also can commonly find a wealth of *subjective* information on any purchase you are considering. Customer reviews of hotels, restaurants, movies, and many other products are common on the web sites that market and sell them. We are truly in an information age when it comes to many purchases.

Health care is not nearly as transparent. If a consumer wants to learn which therapists are most effective or efficient in their city, there simply is no place for them to turn for *objective* information comparing therapists on these metrics. Sure, they can seek out recommendations from friends (as many do), search online (as many do), and read through a variety of therapists' web pages and directory listings (as many do). But objective information that can be used to compare one therapist with another is simply not available.

Making the matter worse, because therapy occurs in private and many clients do not widely discuss their experiences in therapy, it is difficult for prospective clients to get even subjective information on a therapist they are considering contacting. For someone who is even mildly distrustful of therapy or therapists in general – and as we have discussed, there are many such people – the lack of information available about a therapist (beyond the therapist's own marketing material) may only deepen their skepticism.

Little wonder, then, that prospective clients turn to sites like Yelp, HealthGrades, or Angie's List. These sites aggregate client reports of their experience with therapists and other health care providers. While many in health care scoff at these sites (I hear discussion with some frequency from therapists who wished the sites didn't exist at all), how else can a potential client be confident they have made the best choice they could for their care?

Admittedly, in their present form these recommendation sites are far from perfect. Too few people use them to make their overall ratings trustworthy: Only 3 to 4 percent of Internet users in one large study had posted a review of any health care provider or facility online.[204] And of course, the subset of clients inclined to go online and talk about their experience with you may not be a representative group. It's well-established when it comes to online reviews of all kinds that those who are most and least satisfied are far more likely to post reviews than are people from the vast, satisfied-enough middle. It's fully appropriate to warn friends and family members not to take those recommendation sites too seriously when it comes to choosing health care providers. A very limited selection of subjective reports is a poor substitute for more objective information, and arguably worse as a basis for choosing a therapist than no information at all.

But we do the public a disservice by leaving them with nothing but our own proclamations of our greatness. Consumers may benefit from knowing that others found a therapist to be helpful, and the specific thoughts and experiences of other clients. Therapists themselves are often loathe to provide any meaningful information about their practices as we have discussed, leaving prospective clients to rely on their best guesses about how to choose a therapist. It's even possible that widespread use of consumer review sites for therapists could lead to better treatment outcomes, as clients seek out (and are hopefully then able to find) the therapist who is truly the best fit for what they need.

Therapists tend to be more than a little wary of these sites. There are already several sites that specialize in consumer reviews of health care providers (HealthGrades is perhaps the most widely known). Because of the private and confidential nature of the services that health care providers offer, one of the largest challenges is how a therapist should handle bad reviews; in the interest of client confidentiality, we can't challenge negative reviews nor can we even acknowledge whether a particular reviewer was a client. We can, however, take some actions on both individual and collective levels.

Our professional associations can warn consumers about the weaknesses inherent in reviews of therapists on sites like these. We also could add to our professional directories the ability for therapists to endorse and review one another (a feature already prominent on LinkedIn, but not one typically used by consumers when selecting therapists); this would allow prospective clients some meaningful external comments on a practitioner without the ethical quandaries of having clients do the commenting. Individually, if we find ourselves listed on sites like these, many offer the opportunity for practitioners to "claim" their listing – giving you a bit more control over the information consumers see, and sometimes allowing you to post a statement to the effect of, "Like all reputable mental health professionals, I care deeply about your privacy and confidentiality. Therefore I regret that I cannot respond to any comments posted here, regardless of their content. If you would like to speak with me directly, please contact me at [phone number]."

## Innovation, with or without us

Speaking of technology, there are a number of innovations that are poised – or at least trying – to radically change how therapeutic services are conceptualized and delivered. Therapists have shown willingness to adapt to new technologies, as evidenced by the growth of online therapy. But for many therapists, this flexibility has limits, as evidenced by the reaction to services like BetterHelp and Talkspace.

Where technology has the potential to use the principles and practices of psychotherapy to improve people's lives, we essentially have two options: We can be part of the innovation process, or we can be travel agents.

Every aspect of psychotherapy should be open to scientific scrutiny to make sure we are delivering our services in the most efficient and effective way possible. That scrutiny will inevitably support some aspects of our practice and take aim at some sacred cows – consider the research reviewed just in this book on the importance of the therapeutic relationship, and the lack of importance of specific theoretical models in determining outcome.

This kind of close examination is good and necessary. Indeed, in much of health care it is a baseline expectation that all aspects of training and practice are subject to evaluation and, where possible and beneficial, change.

There is a strange tension that emerges, though, when anyone tries to innovate in how therapy services are conceptualized and delivered. If therapy can happen successfully on a street corner, by phone, or on a walk through the park, what's the need for an office? If therapy can happen by text, what's to stop a therapist from copy-pasting the same messages to clients with similar problems at similar stages of therapy? And if what people really want from therapists and counselors is advice, can coaches do that job effectively with far less training than therapists?

Some of this may be simple insecurity. As I mentioned in the discussion of the different therapy professions in Task 1, many of today's younger therapists are given little information about the unique social context that gave rise to their chosen field or the unique philosophical underpinnings that it *doesn't* share with other mental health professions. Common practices like the 50-minute therapy hour, in the therapist's office, talking directly about the problem at hand are treated as givens, so that when these are later questioned, we cling to the way we were taught even if we can't explain *why* we need therapy to work this way.

One example of this shows itself in discussions of the companies seeking to connect clients with therapists through text messaging. BetterHelp, Talkspace, and similar services allow clients to pay a flat monthly fee to be assigned a therapist who will communicate only via text. (In some cases, clients can pay an extra fee for phone or video sessions; the services offered by specific companies vary.) Clients typically can text as often as they like, and therapists respond when they are able.

For clients, such services are incredibly convenient. Most of us have phones on us at all times, so it's easy for a client to text in the specific moment when they are feeling distress. This can be helpful for therapists to properly assess symptoms, as opposed to relying on client retrospective self-report. Clients also can text as much or as little as they would like, more effectively matching "dosage" with need. And, of course, it's far less time-consuming for clients than driving to and from a therapist's office for an hour session each week.

Many therapists are resistant to these companies and others seeking to innovate in how therapy is offered. When I posted an article about Talk-space in a popular Facebook group of therapists, most responses were negative. Several were along the lines of "I would sooner light myself on fire."

No one is going to force you to be involved in that kind of a startup if you don't want to, of course. But these innovations will happen whether we are involved in them or not. Those that succeed can have powerful impacts on the field. And the ones that are both effective and enjoyable for clients can become the expected standard with surprising speed: The number of travel agents declined by two-thirds in less than 20 years, mostly due to travelers booking their own flights online.[205]

## Prove yourself

We can't say we didn't see this coming. In the first edition of *The Heart and Soul of Change: What Works in Therapy*, published in 1999, authors Mark Hubble, Barry Duncan, and Scott Miller predicted that psychotherapists would soon be facing a new era of accountability for their work.[206] Clients, payors, and policymakers would all demand hard evidence that psychotherapy was effective. That era is well underway, and so far we have provided a wealth of the kind of information these parties have demanded. We can demonstrate that therapy works as an overall conclusion and within the contexts of specific problems and populations. Proving the effectiveness of specific models has been helpful in many ways (showing that model-based treatment is superior to no treatment) and enlightening in others (showing that, for most problems, the model of therapy has little to no impact on outcome). The brain research discussed by Siegel, Cozolino, and others explains *why* therapy works. Psychotherapy in general is being held accountable, and it is passing the test with flying colors.

The same cannot be said of therapists, or of therapy training programs – yet. Individual therapists have historically not had to prove their effectiveness in any meaningful or measurable way, and training programs have historically been evaluated more on their inputs (like following a common curriculum) than their outputs (whether they produce competent and effective graduates). But accountability on these levels is coming, and quickly.

Greater accountability is going to wind up closing some graduate programs in psychotherapy. Whether morally right or not, this is the reality. Online universities have already seen steep enrollment drops in the face of increased scrutiny from the federal government, and increased attention to their attrition and job placement rates. Accreditors in the psychotherapy professions are now demanding that programs publish information on programs' costs, completion rates, diversity, license exam pass rates, and employment rates after graduation – information that will likely steer prospective students away from underperforming programs. Even APA-accredited programs in psychology will risk accreditation loss and ultimately closure if they can't place enough of their students in accredited internships – and there aren't enough internships to go around.

The domino effect of these pressures will be interesting to watch. In many ways, the outcomes could be good for our field: Programs may reduce enrollments (by eliminating academically weaker applicants) and adopt higher standards for graduation (to ensure their license exam success data remains strong). Fewer programs and smaller enrollments in existing programs would ease the concern among some therapists that there are simply too many professionals in the field.[207]

These changes in therapist training will necessarily lead to heightened accountability for individual therapists, at least while they are within their training programs. Some programs are already experimenting with structured clinical exercises for students to prove that they can perform specific skills – with those students who fail given additional training.[208] Others are utilizing outcome data on individual therapists to tailor their training and ensure competency before allowing a student to graduate. In this way, programs are slowly transitioning to requiring that students demonstrate not just knowledge (through papers and exams) but measurable clinical effectiveness.

## Continuing competency

The individual therapist accountability described above occurs within the context of graduate training. But establishing that you are a minimally effective practitioner should probably not be something that is done once at the end of your academic training and then forgotten. All of the professional associations in psychotherapy expect therapists to actively maintain their competence through continuing education and training throughout our careers.

There is a movement in regulatory circles to replace traditional continuing education with continuing competency – a form of professional development that involves continuing to be accountable throughout your career. Continuing education requires simply that you be present for a set number of hours of seminars; continuing *competency* requires you to demonstrate that you actually are current with the profession.

Several students and therapists have privately told me that they are anxious about the continuing competency approach. They worry that it might lead to their needing to retake licensing exams every few years, and that they thus might fail to stay current enough to maintain their licensure even after years in practice.

Those aren't necessarily bad things.

Let's preface this discussion by clarifying that it's *highly unlikely* that states would actually adopt re-examinations for licensure spaced out every few years.[209] There is an argument to be made that they should – many states do periodic re-examination for driver's licenses, and it seems logical that maintaining a license to work in private with clients who could be suicidal, homicidal, or otherwise struggling with severe mental illness should perhaps be more difficult than maintaining a license to drive a Honda to the grocery store. But licensing boards know that they would suffer a groundswell of panicked opposition from their licensees if they proposed such a transition.

And let's also acknowledge the problems with license exams that were discussed earlier in this text: As they are today, they *don't* appear to make professionals any safer or more effective. Accountability is only a good thing insofar as we are *measured appropriately* in relation to reasonable standards. But if we limited discussion to the kind of genuinely safety-focused exam I proposed in Task 2 – an exam focused on law, ethics, and crisis intervention, where the standards do frequently change – then the possibility of re-examination every few years starts to have more potential for being a good thing.

But it doesn't matter. It won't happen.

What is more likely instead is that states will transition to a model of continuing competency that requires therapists to assess their own practices, identify areas of needed growth, focus their professional development activities on areas that will foster that growth, and then provide evidence that they actually learned something from those activities. These requirements may lead therapists to roll our eyes or grumble about regulatory over-reach, but they are in fact small and reasonable steps to ensure we can actually demonstrate that we are remaining current in our practices.

You may be wondering whether there is an inconsistency between the demands of continuing competency, which I generally support, and the research discussed under Task 2, which shows that increased training levels have little impact on clinical effectiveness. I don't believe there is, at least not in context of the research on skill development also discussed in that chapter. Simply having your butt in a seat for a set amount of time isn't like-ly to improve your skills or make you a more effective therapist. But deliberate practice on your known areas of weakness will. And a continuing competency approach like the one described above basically is an effort to push therapists into deliberate practice.

# Taking it personally: What you can do

Accountability is as much an individual issue as it is a collective is-sue. Each of us as individuals needs to be able to demonstrate that the work we do is effective, or find a way to get better. If we can't do either of those things, our clients would be best served by our leaving the field. Of course, that should be a very rare finding – the overwhelming majority of therapists are actually quite effective. One of the biggest benefits of taking on ac-countability as a clear professional value would be that it would be much easier to prove that to skeptical clients or a skeptical public. Here's what you can start doing on an individual level right now to improve your prac-tice and help raise the bar for public expectations of us all.

### 1. Gather data on your practice

As therapists, we never have to prove our effectiveness. Ever. That can be chilling: Imagine a doctor going through an entire 40-year career without ever curing a single patient. The doctor would likely be run out of town.

And yet this can absolutely happen in therapy. We can continue practicing outdated or even debunked methods of therapy, we can explain away our treatment failures as unmotivated or poorly matched clients, and we can use good marketing to replace the clients who catch on to our inef-fectiveness with new ones.

At present, there are a number of good, brief ways therapists of all kinds can measure their effectiveness with clients. If you work primarily with a single type of problem, there are brief measures for nearly every specific disorder imaginable. If you work with a variety of problem types, there are a number of tools that evaluate progression toward therapy goals and satisfaction with the therapy process. Even better, many of these instruments can be obtained and used at no cost whatsoever.

Ethical codes are increasingly recognizing the need for us to evaluate our practices in more formal ways than spending a few minutes on a random Thursday thinking about whether we're really doing the best work we can. The American Counseling Association's 2014 Code of Ethics added for the first time a requirement that counselors "continually monitor their effectiveness as professionals and take steps to improve when necessary." The word *continually* is important there, as it makes clear that evaluating yourself once every five years or even once every year is not enough. Nor is examining effectiveness on a case-by-case basis sufficient if counselors are monitoring "their effectiveness as professionals." Larger-scale review is in order. While the ACA Code does not establish the parameters or formality of this type of self-assessment, it does offer a clear expectation that it be done in some way.

Licensing boards are also beginning to require more meaningful evaluation of effectiveness. As discussed earlier, the movement toward "continuing competency" will gradually require more therapists in more states to seek out professional development activities that will improve their performance in areas they determined *based on meaningful evaluation of their practices*.

I say don't wait until you are forced to do this. Starting it now is easy, can be done for free, and will help you become a more effective therapist. There are a number of quick assessments that therapists can use to see whether clients are satisfied with their services and reaching the goals you have set for their therapy:

- Personally, I'm a fan of Miller and Duncan's Session Rating Scale and Outcome Rating Scale (SRS and ORS), which are brief (and I mean *really* brief – four questions each, responded to with hash marks on a scale) and can be applied across all types of clients and problems. There are versions in Spanish and for multiple age groups. In addition to helping you see where you are going right and wrong in therapy, the SRS and ORS are pretty good at predicting therapy dropout. They can provide strong evidence for the effectiveness of your work – or the need for you to get better.[210] An individual license to use the instruments is free.

- The World Health Organization Disability Assessment Schedule (WHODAS) 2.0 is included in the DSM-5 and also freely available online.[211] Its 36 items address functionality across six domains of daily living. It can be used as an outcome measure in therapy, though it tracks the past 30 days and so may not be a good measure for brief approaches.
- The Psychlops, a one-page outcome measure using client-defined goals, is free to use as of September 2015.[212]
- The OQ-45 is a questionnaire that assesses client progress toward outcomes in just a few minutes. It does require payment, but has been extensively validated.[213]
- In addition to these and other specific instruments, there are a number of practice management software programs that include client feedback as a regular part of practice. On an individual basis, they can show you things like when you're at your best. If it turns out clients are happiest with you in the afternoon or evening, that can tell you that you might need coffee before those morning sessions. In an agency setting, they can help you see whether some supervisees have higher client dropout rates than others, as well as other information that can be incredibly valuable in guiding supervision.

You may be surprised at the kind of impact that gathering data can have on your practice. First and foremost, the mere act of gathering client feedback in a systematic way can improve outcomes and help prevent dropouts, supporting clinical effectiveness while earning you additional money.[214] Literally *a few seconds* at the end of each session for a brief data-gathering procedure could mean improved success in therapy for your clients (and, in settings where you are paid by the session, improved income for you). Perhaps this is because clients understand data-gathering as part of a process of accountability, and find accountable therapists to be more trustworthy than unaccountable ones. In any case, when you then go on to *use* that data in a productive way – whether reflecting to clients what they noted and its impact, or making larger-scale changes to your practice – even greater professional success seems likely to result.

If you are under supervision or otherwise an employee within an organization, you may have to push for this kind of data to be gathered. Do it.

You are setting a tone within your organization that accountability is a key part of professional practice.

## 2. Make your data public

There is obviously great value in gathering data about your practice for your own sake, and using it to improve your work. When it comes to having a larger impact on the field, one way to do so is to make your data public. While most professional associations specifically prohibit client testimonials, and there are appropriate concerns with publishing data on any individual clients without their permission,[215] posting *aggregate* data about your practice further supports the idea that therapists should be accountable for their work. It also openly acknowledges to prospective clients that *you* hold yourself accountable for the quality of your work, a valuable marketing edge.

If your practice is small or just getting off the ground, or if you've just started gathering data about your practice, you might think it's not possible to share data about your work. It still can be helpful, though, to post available data on the methods you use. Just bear in mind that many states require any scientific claims about your particular form of therapy be supportable through published, peer-reviewed studies.[216]

Ultimately, the more objective information you can post about your practice, the better. Aggregated information like the number of clients you saw last year, the average number of sessions in completed cases, and the percentage that reported meeting their goals does not violate the confidentiality of any specific client (and even if you had concerns that it would, just add a brief piece to your informed consent document letting them know that you collect and share this information in aggregate form). If your practice is too small for such information to be reliable, then post objective information about the treatment model you use. In short, anything that is objective and can be used to meaningfully compare you with other therapists will be helpful to prospective clients. When we fail to do so, we can't reasonably complain about clients choosing therapists based solely on criteria like price, insurance reimbursement, location, or gender. We haven't given them anything else they can compare.[217]

## 3. Hold your peers to a higher standard

I noted a few pages back that Miller and Hubble described a "culture of excellence" as important to improving clinical outcomes. If you believe in high standards of service in psychotherapy, as I believe most therapists do, you are not bound to wander the desert in search of such an oasis. You can find a culture of excellence, or you can create one.

These cultures, according to Miller and Hubble, have some things in common: They have leaders who insist on high standards and are willing to do the work to implement appropriate measurement tools; they develop a culture of trust where clinicians are comfortable admitting their mistakes and working on areas where they can improve; and they have a common interest in the measurement of performance – they "share and compare" their results.[218] If you adopt these practices to whatever degree possible given your current professional role, others around you are sure to take an interest – and may even want to follow in your footsteps.

Holding your peers to a higher standard involves particular attention to mistakes and failures in therapy, the second trait of cultures of excellence. Recall from Task 4 that therapists observe, on average, more than one ethically questionable act by a colleague each year. Many therapists say they would not address the unethical behavior of a colleague, which is problematic on several levels. It obviously allows for the unethical behavior to continue, creating whatever damage it may create. To the degree that the peer or others in the same clinic know that unethical behavior is being seen and going unchallenged, this fosters a culture of ambivalence – one that I hope you would refuse to be part of.

Gentle and supportive confrontation is a skill, and it is one that you likely have developed fairly well in your clinical work. Nowhere is it more important than in addressing a colleague who is acting outside of accepted professional standards. Often, a single conversation is all it takes to remind a colleague of their professional responsibilities and put them on a course toward more ethical behavior.

It is essential to address unethical behavior when it is observed. Most of the time, though, the failures we deal with are far more mundane: the clients who drop out without warning, or who choose to end therapy without having reached their goals. The leadership and trust necessary for your workplace to become a culture of excellence is built each time you have the courage to openly discuss your own treatment failures, to look at them closely and without defensiveness. Colleagues who see you do this with your own work are much more likely to trust you to help them with their own struggles.

Recall from the beginning of this book that client outcomes in psychotherapy haven't measurably improved in 30 years. Now consider the fact that, based on the research seen throughout this book but particularly in this chapter, we now know of specific practices that *can* improve outcomes. Psychotherapy could take its first leap forward in decades – if we are willing to hold ourselves and our peers accountable as meaningful determinants of change.

# Conclusion:
# Starting today

This book is meant to serve as both a warning and an action plan. Hopefully you see the promise here for what the field of psychotherapy can be when its practitioners take individual responsibility for the well-being of the therapeutic community.

Remember the brighter future for our profession that I hypothesized in the beginning of this book? It is readily available to us if we have the collective courage to go after it. *We can* have a future where the main barrier to entry in the profession is skill and not wealth. *We can* successfully train therapists just as effectively, in less time and at lower cost. *We can* treat science as integral to our work and necessary for us to justify our rates – we find in the literature today ample support for psychotherapy's power. And *we can* make psychotherapy more effective than it has been in generations with basic measurement and accountability.

The time is right for a resurgence in psychotherapy's stature, if we are wise in how we approach the opportunities available to us. As I mentioned in the Introduction, the public is growing more skeptical of the claims of drugmakers. Consumers are actively seeking out knowledge about mental health care online – therapists and our professional associations can and should be leaders in providing that information.

By taking a number of very specific and focused steps, you can improve your practice while raising the profile of psychotherapy as a whole. The five tasks in this book – the four outlined in each of the previous chapters, plus the task of *taking it personally* that underlies each – are the way to do it. They don't require you to rely on the help of others or wait for those in positions of power to make better choices. They are all up to you. While I would hope *every* professional would readily take on these tasks, every step you take toward each one is likely to help your practice while nudging the lot of us forward.

# Starting today

Each task can be carried out through focused actions that actually require very little time or money. Let's review your action plan here, with very specific steps to get started if you're not sure how to do so. For each of these, you certainly can add other actions to the list below. These are just suggestions, and there are many ways to reach the goals I've put forward.

## Task 1: Clarify our purpose and values

- **Clarify your purpose and values.**
    - List, *in order*, **the values** you seek to uphold in your work. This can be a challenging exercise, as it gets easy to simply make a list of words with which you have good associations, or which seem to be socially valued. "Honesty" is a good example. Many of us value honesty, but if you would tell a friend "you look great!" when you know they don't, you are showing that you value kindness above honesty. If you are having trouble deciding which value ranks ahead of another, consider a situation where the two would conflict.
    - **Draft a mission statement for your practice**, if you haven't done so already. It should be just a sentence or two, and take the effort to make it specific enough that it meaningfully sets you apart from the therapist down the street.

- **Make your values clear to prospective clients**
    - **Post your mission statement on your web site.** If you did well at crafting a statement that reflects clearly on your specific practice, this will clearly differentiate you from other therapists, and show prospective clients what they can expect from working with you.
    - **Review your marketing materials from the eyes of a prospective client. Have at least one non-therapist friend review your materials as well.** Can they pick up on your mission and values from your materials? If not, adjust your materials accordingly.

## Task 2: Fix therapist training

- **Let money be an explicit factor in decision-making.**
    - **Meet with a financial planner**. Map out where you would like to be in terms of income within the next 5 to

10 years. If you are not making enough in your current position to get there, it would be worth considering transitioning jobs.

- o **Have a conversation with students and new professionals about money.** It is something of a taboo topic in some circles, and new professionals sometimes think that because our profession exists to help others, it is somehow selfish or inappropriate to express our own financial concerns. Regardless of where you are in your career, having an open conversation about financial issues can help challenge this perception.
- o This also gives you the opportunity to **steer students and new professionals toward smart financial decisions.** While an individual's context matters, typically advise against taking unpaid internships unless the intern has the financial means to work comfortably as a volunteer. Advise students or prospective students against taking on massive student loan debt unless they have a clear plan to pay it back.
- o If you're in private practice, and if it is consistent with your purpose and values, **raise your fee.** Obviously you will want to consider market factors in this decision, and if you are changing fees for current clients, provide them with ample notice in accordance with your profession's code of ethics. But many therapists' reluctance to charge more seems to stem more from guilt than from a realistic, if perhaps cold, calculation of how their financial goals fit with the local market.

- **Fight for those behind you**
  - o **Write a letter about your experience as an incoming professional.** Highlight the successes and the struggles you experienced. Offer specific suggestions for what could be done better to improve the experience of others coming into the profession today. Send that letter to your state licensing board, or even better, read it at a licensing board meeting. You may be surprised at how responsive the board is to what you have to offer – and

at how few other therapists attend to the new professional pipeline once they are through it.

- **Supervise**
  - If you're not already supervising, **take a supervisor training course** and start the process of meeting your state's supervision standards.
  - If you are already supervising, **integrate deliberate practice into your supervision.** Focus on practicing a specific skill, several times, in a supervision session – ideally a skill that the supervisee has not been doing well. When reviewing video, have the supervisee show only a 5-10 minute clip where they feel they need the most assistance.
  - Going along with both this task and Task 4, **use a robust evaluation process for your supervisees.** This should involve your rating of their skills, their own rating of their skills, and objective data on how their clients are doing.

## Task 3: Embrace science

- **Be a skeptic, not a cynic**
  - **Meaningfully assess your ways of knowing.** Do you place the most faith in your clinical experience, your personal experience, scientific findings, religion, or something else? In keeping with the discussion of values in Task 1, this will likely be a helpful thing for your clients to know about you.
  - **Practice evaluating articles about research.** Criticizing means assessing both strengths and weaknesses, and it's a skill set that improves with practice. Find a recent news story about a research study relevant to your work. Pay attention to what the study does and doesn't report, and see whether you can draft in a sentence or two how you would describe that study to a colleague or to an interested family member.

- **Be an evidence-based therapist**
  - o **Check in on the knowledge base.** Whatever your particular area of clinical practice is, look for recent research on that area in Google Scholar, EBSCOhost, or another research database to which you have access. You can limit search results to only those articles published since a certain year, so set this to the time you last checked in on the research in your area of practice. What's new since then?
  - o **Work on your biases.** We all have them to some degree. Given the known links between therapist bias and clinical outcome, any steps you take to reduce your biases are likely to pay off in the quality of care you provide. Education, supervision, and your own therapy are all good places to do this work.

- **Use a map**
  - o **Replace words like "eclectic" and "integrative" with more specific descriptions of your work.** There was a time when eclecticism was trendy among psychotherapists, a way of saying that we are free thinkers who don't conform to the strictures of a single way of thinking about our work. In concept, that is indeed valuable. In practice, however, eclecticism too often seems to be the calling card of therapists who can't define what they are doing or why they are doing it. Telling your colleagues or clients that you draw from a wide variety of theoretical approaches doesn't actually say anything about what you do. Surely you have a conceptual framework that organizes therapy, that tells you where you have been with a client, where you are, and how to get to where you are headed next. It may be based on a specific theoretical model, or it may be one you've adapted over time through clinical experience. Either way, colleagues and clients benefit from knowing in a clear and specific way how you think about therapy.
  - o **Organize your treatment.** This may be a requirement where you are working, but even if it is not, it is good

practice. Pick a case you are working with, and in just a sentence or two, write out (1) your conceptualization of the issue at hand, (2) your treatment goals, and (3) your treatment methods. Do they all logically connect? If not, you may want to revisit your treatment plan, making sure that you and your client are on the same page.

## Task 4: Become accountable

### • Gather data

o **Download the SRS and ORS, the WHODAS, or a similar instrument.** Integrating it into your practice to gather data on treatment outcomes is easy. In the case of the SRS, it can also be used to predict and prevent early termination.

o If you have a small practice, **do a review of cases closed in the past year.** Depending on the size of your practice and how you gather data, you may need to set aside a couple of hours for this. The specific data points may vary based on the nature of your practice, but calculate data on questions like:

▪ How did the clients find you?

▪ How many sessions did they attend?

▪ Did they reach the goals as set at the beginning of treatment?

▪ Were they satisfied with the services you provided?

And of course, any other questions that can help grow and improve your practice. Within each of these, you may also want to keep track of whether there were meaningful differences based on client demographics – for example, whether you were more effective with male clients than with female ones. You may also want to consider using practice management software that can gather and tabulate this data for you on a regular basis.

- **Make your data public**
  - o **Add aggregate data to your marketing materials.** "Our clinic helped 557 clients reach their goals last year" is a powerful statement that can help prospective clients build trust in your clinic. "More than 90% of my clients reported satisfaction with my services last year" is also helpful. "I've treated more than 1,000 clients experiencing depression" may be a more valuable statement to a prospective client struggling with depression than anything you might say about your chosen methods. Be truthful and current in your reporting, and be careful not to include anything that could be considered misleading or personally identifiable, of course. (Note that some places have specific advertising laws governing claims of effectiveness, so make sure your advertising is legally and ethically compliant.)

- **Hold your peers to a high standard**
  - o **Help someone who isn't living up to professional expectations.** *We all* know someone like this, who may be highly ethical and professional in general but is dropping the ball in one or two specific areas. (It's also true that for many of us, that someone – or at least one of those someones – is us.) Practice addressing this in a way that is respectful and understanding, but direct: The impact of their behavior isn't just limited to their clients. Simply ineffective therapy should be improved through practice and training; doing so requires that we first understand what it is we're doing wrong, which often requires gentle but specific feedback from others who have seen our work. Unethical or unprofessional behaviors, meanwhile, are contagious. Any time a client, a student, or a supervisee witnesses a professional falling short of the standards we share, the respect they give to others in the field falls a bit. These behaviors do harm to *all of us* by lowering the reputation of *every* practitioner. By pushing for a higher standard with one

person, you are pushing for changes in behavior that help us all.

As I hope you can see, these are not pie-in-the-sky tasks. You don't need anyone else to help you with any of them. Many take just a few minutes and have little or no cost. And by doing them, you are likely to improve your own outcomes while simultaneously having a positive impact on the entire field.

---

**These are not pie-in-the-sky tasks. Many take just a few minutes and have little or no cost.**

---

If your circumstances allow you to do only one or two things of the above list, that is still far better than doing none of them. I was serious about starting today: Go back through that list, including any other tasks you may have added to it, and *pick one or two tasks that you can do within the next 24 hours* to get the ball rolling.

Ultimately, I would encourage you to do all of these that you reasonably can. I will happily admit to being pushy here. Each of these things that you do can help you individually have a sustainable and successful practice. It also helps *me* individually, and it helps us as members of the psychotherapy family, by raising prospective clients' impressions of therapists and of the services we offer.

I also would like to add two final tasks to your list.

## Join your professional association

I don't think you should join your association because it's good. As discussed in Task 1, I believe professional associations have, in a good-faith effort to gain membership by focusing on member benefits, lost sight of their larger purpose of promoting the profession *by serving the public*. I think you should join your association because it's in trouble. Criticism from the outside will not help it to be better. Change in professional associations occurs from within, when members raise their voices to demand change and become an active part of that change.

Young adults, including those coming into the therapy profession, have shown time and again that they are not interested in joining any institution – a professional association, a church, a political party – just for the sake of being part of that institution.[219] Professional associations in particular have grown worried about what this will mean for their membership as potential members shy away from what some researchers call affiliative behavior.

But what I see in my students and colleagues, and is reflected in research, is more complex than a simple resistance to joining stuff. It's a hunger to be part of a *mission*. New therapists don't join a group just because it's available, or even because they're told they're supposed to. They create and join organizations whose cause they believe in and want to support, and where they see that their involvement makes a real difference.[220] If they don't see that in a church, a political party, a professional organization, or any other institution, they won't join it.

Professional associations in mental health are dropping the ball by trying to gain new members through a focus on member benefits. I've heard several association staff people talk about the "value proposition" in joining an association, essentially referring to the "bang for your buck" that one gets for their member dues. It seems to me that a lot of new therapists care much more about what they can do for their clients and communities than about what the association can do for them.

Looking historically at professional associations, that is what they once were – an opportunity to support and advance the standing of one's field by giving more to the public than you would receive in return. Today, with the psychotherapy professions well-established and the initial fights to exist having concluded, associations are doing a poor job defining for potential members what the mission is that they would be serving by joining today. *We'll advocate for your profession* is too vague to inspire action. *We'll help you market your practice* is fine as far as it goes, but probably not worth hundreds of dollars a year for the poor returns most associations' therapist-finder directories offer. Magazines, scholarly journals, and brochures about common problems are also helpful, but most of the knowledge contained therein is accessible online. Many of the therapists dropping out of associations don't view the cost-effectiveness of their membership as a question of *Are you giving me my money's worth?* Instead, I hear over and over again different versions of *Does my membership make a difference?* And all too often, the apparent answer is "no."

You can fix this, but nothing will change if you grumble from the outside about how inactive your professional association is. The way to fix it is to get involved and demand change from within. I spoke in the beginning of this book about how often I have been surprised at the difference one person can make in creating change at a systemic level. There is no reason at all why that one person should not be you.

# Be an activist therapist

Only about one in every 10 US adults has a master's or doctoral degree.[221] Of those degrees, of course, the overwhelming majority are in fields unrelated to psychotherapy. Recent estimates suggest that only one out of roughly every 480 US adults is a licensed psychotherapist.[222]

With our high education, high standards for licensure, and specialized roles, we have earned a position as society's experts in mental health and behavior change. Far too many of us, however, hope to achieve the benefits of that status without taking on its responsibilities – to hold meaningful knowledge and use it to guide our clients, to stand up for what we believe to be good for the community around us, to be accountable for the quality and success of our work.

We want high pay, but we don't confront the woman distracting everyone from Linehan's talk.

When you find yourself in a room without a leader, *you have a responsibility to become that leader*. The field of psychotherapy is in dire need of leaders to pull us away from the path we find ourselves on, a path of steady erosion of public confidence in our work. You don't need to be a lobbyist, a licensing board member, a professional association board member, or an academic to lead your colleagues. You just need to do your job well, and to do the tasks outlined in this book.

Consider how many of the specific activities described here are about taking a public stand:

- Make your values clear to prospective clients (from Task 1)
- Fight for those behind you (from Task 2)
- Use a map (from Task 3)
- Make your data public (from Task 4)

These are all tasks you take on at an individual level, but which can be rightly described as public-facing. They will draw prospective clients to you, giving you a competitive advantage in your local market, and also "raise the bar" in terms of what clients learn to expect from professional therapists. They will cause you to be seen as a leader in your professional community.

Here, I'm asking you to go a step further. Protest that which is not working for our profession, and loudly champion what is.

## Protest that which is not working in our profession, and loudly champion what is.

Defining yourself as an activist therapist means not only setting a high bar for professional behavior, but fighting for what you believe is good and right in the profession against those who would drag us down. It means taking the specialized knowledge and status you have rightly earned and putting them to use for the benefit of those around you. It means meeting the obligations that come with being a professional.

More to the point, though, it means *being a therapist*. Back in Task 1, we discussed the *professional* part of being a professional therapist. Here, I ask you to consider the *therapist* part. When I ask students and colleagues what it means to be a therapist, I hear responses like *healer* and *change agent*. I agree with both of those. You may or may not agree with the word *expert* (I do), but certainly being a therapist means possessing uncommon skills at emotional connection, at understanding and changing behavior.

Being a therapist, in the most fundamental sense of the word, means more than simply being a witness to problematic behavior, in the way so many were at Linehan's presentation. It means taking active responsibility for changing it.

Being a therapist means pushing for change even when others lack the courage to do so.

Being a therapist means owning your role as a leader, and honoring the exchange you make with the community around you for professional status.

Our profession is slowly eroding, doing particular harm to new professionals. It is hard to say how long this erosion will continue, how long we as a collective group might remain lost in the proverbial woods. You can lead us out. I hope and expect that if you take the actions outlined here, others will follow you. But if they do not, you can be one of those left standing. First, you have to stand.

# Notes

[1] Psychotherapy's effect size is drawn from Wampold, B. E. (2001).

[2] Stice, E., Shaw, H., & Marti, C. N. (2006). A meta-analytic review of obesity prevention programs for children and adolescents: The skinny on interventions that work. *Psychological Bulletin, 132*(5), 667-691. Available online at http://www.ncbi.nlm.nih.gov/pmc/articles/PMC1876697/

[3] Wampold, B. E. (2007). The humanistic (and effective) treatment. *American Psychologist, 62*(9), 857-873.

[4] Chiles, J. A., Lambert, M. J., & Hatch, A. L. (1999). The impact of psychological interventions on medical cost offset: A meta-analytic review. *Clinical Psychology, 6*(2), 204–219.

[5] Washington State Institute for Public Policy (2007). *Evidence-based juvenile offender programs: Program description, quality assurance, and cost.* Olympia, WA: Author. Available online at http://www.wsipp.wa.gov/ReportFile/986/Wsipp_Evidence-Based-Juvenile-Offender-Programs-Program-Description-Quality-Assurance-and-Cost_Full-Report.pdf

[6] For psychotherapy: Wampold, B. E. (2001). *The great psychotherapy debate: Model, method, and findings.* New York: Erlbaum. There has been a fair amount of debate about this number, but even highly conservative estimates of therapy's typical effect size place it in the 0.4-0.6 range, still greater than SSRIs for depression and well above the other interventions listed. Of course, that SSRI effect size itself has been quite controversial over the years. See Vohringer, P. A., & Ghaemi, S. N. (2011). Solvng the antidepressant efficacy question? Effect sizes in major depressive disorder. *Clinical Therapeutics, 33*(12), B49-B61. Available online at http://www.ncbi.nlm.nih.gov/pmc/articles/PMC3242920/ . I've used the 0.31 effect size landed on by Turner, Matthews, Linardatos, Tell, & Rosenthal (2008) here. For medication treatment for adolescent substance abuse: Tanner-Smith, E. E., Wilson, S. J., & Lipsey, M. W. (2013). The comparative effectiveness of outpatient treatment for adolescent substance abuse: A meta-analysis. *Journal of Substance Abuse Treatment, 44*(2), 145-158. Available online at http://www.ncbi.nlm.nih.gov/pmc/articles/PMC3477300/ . For childhood obesity prevention programs: Stice, E., Shaw, H., & Marti, C. N. (2006). A

meta-analytic review of obesity prevention programs for children and adolescents: The skinny on interventions that work. *Psychological Bulletin, 132*(5), 667-691. Available online at http://www.ncbi.nlm.nih.gov/pmc/articles/PMC1876697/

[7] Cozolino, L. (2010). *The neuroscience of psychotherapy: Healing the social brain (2nd ed).* New York: Norton. Quotes are from pp. 341-342.

[8] For a good, succinct history of mental health parity laws in the US, I like this issue brief from Mental Health America: http://www.mentalhealthamerica.net/issues/issue-brief-parity

[9] We'll revisit some of this technology, and how therapists are reacting to it, later in the book.

[10] Available online at http://www.samhsa.gov/data/sites/default/files/2k12MH_Findings/2k12MH_Findings/NSDUHmhfr2012.htm#sec2-4

[11] Olfsun, M., & Marcus, F. C. (2010). National trends in outpatient psychotherapy. *American Journal of Psychiatry, 167*(12), 1456-1463.

[12] Olfsun, M., & Marcus, F. C. (2010). National trends in outpatient psychotherapy. *American Journal of Psychiatry, 167*(12), 1456-1463.

[13] The BLS data extrapolates full-time salaries from reported hourly wages. In that way it includes part-time practitioners, but may overestimate what full-time workers actually make. It also thus fails to account for under-employment (i.e., therapists who are working fewer hours than they would like to be). Also, the BLS data here doesn't perfectly overlay with licensure. I've used the following BLS categories: Psychologists (19-3031 Clinical, Counseling, and School Psychologists); MFTs (21-1013 Marriage and Family Therapists); Counselors (21-1014 Mental Health Counselors); LCSWs (21-1023 Mental Health and Substance Abuse Social Workers). They appear to offer the best available data for psychotherapists in clinical practice. You could argue that means here are not the best measure, since they can be dragged upward by a few outliers at the high end, but medians show similar trends. Adjusted for inflation, the *median* salaries for all four groups were lower in 2014 than they had been in 2007.

[14] American Psychological Assocation (2010). Available online at http://www.apa.org/monitor/2010/04/salaries.aspx

[15] Harris Interactive (2009). Depression survey initiative. Available online at http://www.nami.org/getattachment/About-NAMI/Publications/Surveys/NAMIDepressionReportFINAL.pdf

[16] American Psychological Assocation (2010). Available online at http://www.apa.org/monitor/2010/04/salaries.aspx

[17] Trauer, J. M., Qian, M. Y., Doyle, J. S., Rajaratnam, S. M. W., & Cunnington, D. (2015). Cognitive behavioral therapy for chronic insomnia: A systematic review and meta-analysis. *Annals of Internal Medicine.* Published online June 9, 2015; not yet in print. Available online at http://annals.org/article.aspx?articleid=2301405

[18] Harvard Health Letter (2011 June 1). Drugs in the water. Available online at http://www.health.harvard.edu/newsletter_article/drugs-in-the-water

[19] If you're wondering, New Zealand is the other country that allows direct-to-consumer advertising of prescription medication.

[20] For a nice roundup of the issue, see Silberman, S. (2009 August 24). Placebos are getting more effective. Drugmakers are desperate to know why. *Wired.* Available at http://archive.wired.com/medtech/drugs/magazine/17-09/ff_placebo_effect?currentPage=all

[21] Gaudiano, B. A., & Miller, I. W. (2013). The evidence-based practice of psychotherapy: Facing the challenges that lie ahead. *Clinical Psychology Review, 33*(5), 813-824.

[22] Ferro, S. (2013 August 21). 3 ways to save psychotherapy. *Popular Science.* Available online at http://www.popsci.com/science/article/2013-08/3-ways-save-psychotherapy

[23] Frosch, D. L., & Grande, D. (2010). Direct-to-consumer advertising of prescription drugs. *LDI Issue Brief, 15*(3), 1-4.

[24] Wood, K. S., & Cromley, M. L. (2014). Then and now: Examining how consumer communication and attitudes of direct-to-consumer pharmaceutical advertising have changed in the last decade. *Health Communication, 29*(8), 814-825.

[25] McHugh, R. K., Whitton, S. W., Peckham, A. D., Welge, J. A., & Otto, M. W. (2015). Patient preference for psychological vs. pharmacological treatment of psychiatric disorders: A meta-analytic review. *Journal of Clinical Psychiatry, 74*(6), 595-602. Available online at http://www.ncbi.nlm.nih.gov/pmc/articles/PMC4156137/pdf/nihms-623724.pdf

[26] National Alliance on Mental Illness (2011). *State mental health cuts: The continuing crisis.* Available online at

http://www2.nami.org/ContentManagement/ContentDisplay.cfm?ContentFil eID=147763 . To be fair, that $1.6b number could be mildly overstated. California slashed more than $175 million from its general fund for mental health services between the 2009 and 2012 fiscal years, but had a separate stream of funding for mental health that is not part of general funds. Some other states also pull mental health funding from sources other than their general funds.

[27] Marley, P., Stein, J., & Kissinger, M. (2014 January 22). Senate sends bills to Scott Walker to improve mental health treatment. *Milwaukee Journal Sentinel.* Available online at http://www.jsonline.com/news/statepolitics/senate-to-take-up-mental-health-treatment-measures-wednesday-b99186659z1-241518411.html

[28] Friedman, R. A. (2015 July 17). Psychiatry's identity crisis. *New York Times,* page SR5. Available online at http://www.nytimes.com/2015/07/19/opinion/psychiatrys-identity-crisis.html

[29] Insel, T. (2014 February 27). Director's blog: A new approach to clinical trials. Available online at http://www.nimh.nih.gov/about/director/2014/a-new-approach-to-clinical-trials.shtml

[30] Bogenschneider, K., Olson, J. R., Mills, J., & Linney, K. D. (2011). How can we connect research with state policymaking? Lessons from the Wisconsin Family Impact Seminars. In K. Bogenschneider (Ed.), *Family policy matters: How policymaking affects families and what professionals can do (2nd ed.),* pp. 245-276. New York: Routledge. If you're interested in how professionals can better inform policymakers about our work, this entire text – now on its third edition – is fantastic.

[31] For a nice rundown of the research on this, see Kessler, R., & Stafford, D. (2008). Primary care is the de facto mental health system. In R. Kessler & D. Stafford (Eds.), *Collaborative medicine case studies,* pp. 9-21. New York: Springer.

[32] Cuijsters, P., Reynolds III, C. F., Donker, T., Li, J., Andersson, G., & Beekman, A. (2012). Personalized treatment of adult depression: Medication, psychotherapy, or both? A systematic review. *Depression and Anxiety, 29*(10), 855-864.

[33] Farberman, R. K. (1997). Public attitudes about psychologists and mental health care: Research to guide the American Psychological Associa-

tion public education campaign. *Professional Psychology: Research and Practice, 28*(2), 128-136.

[34] Bram, A. D. (1997). Perceptions of psychotherapy and psychotherapists: Implications from a study of undergraduates. *Professional Psychology: Research and Practice, 28*(2), 170-178.

[35] Orchowski, L. M., Spickard, B. A., & McNamara, J. R. (2006). Cinema and the valuing of psychotherapy: Implications for clinical practice. *Professional Psychology: Research and Practice, 37*(5), 506-514. This and other studies of media's influence on the public's views of therapists draw heavily from Schneider, I. (1987). The theory and practice of movie psychiatry. *American Journal of Psychiatry, 144*(8), 996–1002.

[36] Vogel, D. L., Gentile, D. A., & Kaplan, S. A. (2008). The influence of television on willingness to seek therapy. *Journal of Clinical Psychology, 64*(3), 276-295.

[37] Beauchamp, T. L., & Childress, J. F. (2009). *Principles of biomedical ethics (6th ed.).* New York: Oxford University Press.

[38] Keeton ultimately lost her suit against Augusta State University. Eastern Michigan University reached a settlement with Ward, without reinstating her to the university. I've written about these cases on multiple occasions at psychotherapynotes.com if you're interested in learning more about either one, or about the religious freedom legislation proposed partly as a result of these cases.

[39] Shulte, J. M. (1990). The morality of influencing in counseling. *Counseling and Values, 34*(2), 103-118. Shulte is, of course, neither the first nor the last to make this argument; it's a consensus opinion in psychotherapy at this point. But Shulte frames it in a way that I find useful and you may as well.

[40] I'm keenly aware of how off-putting this whole conversation may be to my friends in the psychoanalytic community, and I'd like to offer an olive branch here. If you're a psychoanalyst, there is a *very* clear professional value against advice-giving, one that is deeply ingrained in the theory of change psychoanalysts subscribe to. I still think psychoanalysts advise, or at lease that their words and actions will be taken that way. But psychoanalysts have a *far* better argument for attempting to remain neutral than do postmodern therapists, whose theoretical argument against advice-giving falls flat in the face of the postmodern idea that therapy should be a collaborative

effort. (I discuss this postmodern quandary later in the book.) Advising is not imposing, at least in most cases.

[41] Practitioners from some areas of psychotherapy or counseling who are currently battling for their own independent licensure standards, such as drug and alcohol counselors, may argue that they are still in the stage of fighting for professional recognition. But they are generally not fighting for professional *definition*; there are existing certification programs, ethical standards, training opportunities, and professional associations actively serving these groups.

[42] Farberman, R. K. (1997). Public attitudes about psychologists and mental health care: Research to guide the American Psychological Association public education campaign. *Professional Psychology: Research and Practice, 28*(2), 128-136.

[43] http://www.counseling.org/about-us/aca-infographic/

[44] Consensus definition of counseling, available online at www.counseling.org/20-20/index.aspx

[45] I could give you a page full of specific references here, but will instead refer you to one author: Russ Crane. He and his research team have used large data sets from insurance providers to examine differences in mental health treatment based on provider type, finding very few meaningful differences.

[46] And the histories of the professions are fascinating; if you're reading this and thinking that I didn't do justice to the history of your professional group, rest assured I didn't do justice to any of them. That's the price of keeping this section short. But the histories are well worth a deeper dive that closely examines the social and historical context of the development of each profession.

[47] Chiles, J. A., Lambert, M. J., & Hatch, A. L. (1999). The impact of psychological interventions on medical cost offset: A meta-analytic review. *Clinical Psychology, 6*, 204–219.

[48] There are even groups of therapists that have sprung up to take sides on issues like these, such as the National Registry of Marriage Friendly Therapists at http://www.marriagefriendlytherapists.com/ . Also, as an aside here, it's interesting to check for gender bias in how you approach cases like these. Would your therapeutic response be different if it was Annalee, and not Lex, who was considering leaving? If so, why?

[49] I'm a fan of Bill Doherty's *Soul Searching: Why Therapy Must Promote Moral Responsibility*, which addresses this particular issue exceptionally well.

[50] In the interest of full disclosure, I am by no means neutral on this. I think reparative "therapy" is an abhorrent practice that has no place among professionals licensed to serve the public – in addition to being a pseudo-therapeutic embodiment of homophobia, it also appears to be quite dangerous, particularly when applied to children. Those who practice it sometimes cite religious principles and freedoms (either their own or those of clients and their parents) as justification for doing so, but this argument falls flat for me. Our professional community should not and presumably would not accept a form of therapy that embodies racism or xenophobia, and I fail to see how this is any different. I represented the California Division of the American Association for Marriage and Family Therapy in our work on the legislative language that ultimately was signed into law, and in our support of the law in the court challenges that followed.

[51] For clarity's sake, however, I should emphasize that I do not support a choice to take losses *in the scope of practice* of each of the professions represented in the field of psychotherapy. Psychologists, psychiatrists, family therapists, counselors, and social workers are fully competent to – and forgive the legalese here, but it's necessary – assess, diagnose and treat the full range of mental and emotional disorders. The differences between us are found in the foci of treatment and the philosophical lenses through which we do this work, not the scope of problems we are capable of working on.

[52] ACA and AAMFT have both voted on major restructuring proposals in the past few years, and APA has expressed similar concerns. Even the American Psychiatric Association has been accused of rushing DSM development out of financial concerns.

[53] Frances, A. (2013). *Saving normal.* New York: HarperCollins. This quote is from page 223.

[54] Hoffman, D. H., Carter, D. J., Viglucci Lopez, C. R., Benzmiller, H. L., Guo, A. X., Yasir Latifi, S., & Craig, D. C. (2015). Independent review relating to APA ethics guidelines, national security interrogations, and torture. Washington, DC: APA via Sidley Austin LLP. Available online at http://www.apa.org/independent-review/APA-FINAL-Report-7.2.15.pdf

[55] To see the 2009 APA Ethics Committee statement on the issue, visit http://www.apa.org/ethics/programs/statement/torture-code.aspx . In the

wake of the Hoffman report, this internal battle continues. Some members of the APA's Division 19, the Society for Military Psychology, argue that having psychologists present for harsh interrogations can actually help *prevent* human rights violations. For a brief synopsis of key issues written before the Hoffman report was released, see Reisner, S. (2014 December 12). CIA on the couch: Why there would have been no torture without psychologists. *Slate.* Available online at http://www.slate.com/articles/news_and_politics/politics/2014/12/psycholog ists_role_in_the_cia_s_torture_why_these_medical_professionals.single.ht ml

[56] The organization is the California Association of Marriage and Family Therapists (CAMFT). In the interest of full disclosure, I've worked with CAMFT staff on a number of policy issues in California, and I know some of their current board members. I am not a member of the organization.

[57] I have a particular interest in policy work, which stems from my systemic training as a family therapist. From what I've seen, no author makes the case for the importance of therapists (of all types) doing this work as well as Karen Bogenschnieder, whose *Family Policy Matters* is now on its third edition.

[58] Palmer, B. (2014 March 13). Should it really take 14 years to become a doctor? *Slate.* Available online at http://www.slate.com/articles/health_and_science/medical_examiner/2014/0 3/physician_shortage_should_we_shorten_medical_education.single.html

[59] Stein, D. M., & Lambert, M. J. (1995). Graduate training in psychotherapy: Are therapy outcomes enhanced? *Journal of Consulting and Clinical Psychology, 63*(2), 182-196.

[60] For example, this study found that lay counselors could be quickly and easily trained to effectively implement behavioral interventions: Dewing, S., Mathews, C., Cloete, A., Schaay, N., Simbayi, L., & Louw, J. (2014). Lay counselors' ability to deliver counseling for behavior change. *Journal of Consulting and Clinical Psychology, 82*(1), 19-29.

[61] Stein and Lambert (1995) offer the best example of this – once studies that conflated satisfaction with effectiveness are removed from consideration, their meta-analysis is left with very few that still connect experience and effectiveness in any meaningful way; those that do aren't comparing the somewhat-seasoned with the highly-seasoned, they're comparing the seasoned with the brand-new. Stein, D. M., & Lambert, M. J.

(1995). Graduate training in psychotherapy: Are therapy outcomes enhanced? *Journal of Consulting and Clinical Psychology, 63*(2), 182-196.

[62] http://www.apa.org/workforce/publications/grad-98/table-27.pdf

[63] Education cost inflation data from http://inflationdata.com/Inflation/Inflation_Articles/Education_Inflation.asp

[64] http://www.apa.org/workforce/publications/11-grad-study/financial.aspx

[65] https://trends.collegeboard.org/student-aid/figures-tables/average-undergraduate-debt-graduate-debt-and-total-debt-graduate-degree-recipients-2007-08

[66] http://www.finaid.org/calculators/scripts/loanpayments.cgi

[67] As of this writing, the interest rate for unsubsidized direct federal loans for graduate study was 5.84%, and the interest rate for direct federal PLUS loans was 6.84%. Current rates can be found at https://studentaid.ed.gov/sa/types/loans/interest-rates

[68] The calculations I made at http://www.finaid.org/ carry a number of assumptions with them. I didn't include any loan servicing fees, since they can vary so widely by lender, though those can quickly add up. If you're paying fees in addition to interest, that needs to be considered. I also used the calculator's numbers for applying 10% of the borrower's gross income to loan repayment, which corresponds with a debt-to-income ratio of 1.6. Depending on your expense levels, you may be able to afford using a higher percentage of income for debt service, but as the calculator notes, "you may experience some financial difficulty." Most programs use higher thresholds (that is, you would need to be making significantly less than the numbers I use here) when defining economic "hardship" for the purposes of payment deferral eligibility.

[69] Some cautionary notes about the BLS data are in order. First of all, their employment categories do not perfectly correlate with license categories; for the analysis here I've used the BLS categories of Mental Health Counselors (21-1014); Clinical, Counseling, and School Psychologists (19-3031); Marriage and Family Therapists (21-1013), and Mental Health and Substance Abuse Social Workers (21-1023). These are the closest parallels to licensure. In addition, the BLS calculates the average annual wage by surveying on *hourly* wages and then multiplying the mean hourly wage by 2,080. There are benefits and drawbacks to that approach. It keeps the mean from being dragged down by part-time workers, but also arguably overesti-

mates what the average person in each profession actually makes, since many do work part-time. It's hard to tell whether the hourly wages of part-timers are higher, lower, or similar when compared with hourly wages of those who actually do work full-time.

[70] See endnote 13 for some important cautions about BLS data. If you're wondering about the apparent differences between these numbers and those in the salary chart in the introduction, it's simply the difference between means and medians. I used means for showing trends in the chart in the introduction, but for offering current raw numbers here, medians seemed the better choice.

[71] Christie, L. (2014 June 1). Millennials squeezed out of buying a home. Available online at http://money.cnn.com/2014/06/01/real_estate/millennials-squeezed-out/

[72] American Student Assistance (2013). Life delayed: The impact of student debt on the daily lives of young Americans. Available online at http://www.asa.org/site/assets/files/2205/life_delayed.pdf

[73] Stamm, K., et al. (2015 June). *Monitor on Psychology, 46*(6), 15. Available online at http://www.apa.org/monitor/2015/06/datapoint.aspx

[74] Stamm, K., et al. (2015 June). *Monitor on Psychology, 46*(6), 15. Available online at http://www.apa.org/monitor/2015/06/datapoint.aspx

[75] Though the data is a little out of date, this slide set from APA's Center for Workforce Studies is nicely detailed: http://www.apa.org/workforce/presentations/2011/rmpa-handout.pdf

[76] The Institute for College Access and Success (TICAS) produced this data, including useful state-by-state estimates and policy recommendations: http://www.ticas.org/files/pub/classof2012.pdf

[77] Whitaker, T. (2008). *In the red: Social workers and educational debt.* Washington, DC: National Association of Social Workers Center for Workforce Studies. Available online at http://workforce.socialworkers.org/whatsnew/swanddebt.pdf

[78] I support this as an educational requirement, by the way. I don't think that time as a client should count toward licensure, but it can be very helpful for both personal and professional growth.

[79] Wheeler, S., & Cushway, D. (2012). Supervision and clinical psychology: History and development. In I. Fleming and L. Steen (Eds.), *Supervision and clinical psychology: Theory, practice, and perspectives (2nd ed.)*, pp. 11-22. New York: Routledge.

[80] Flexner, A. (1910). *Medical education in the United States and Canada: A report to the Carnegie Foundation for the Advancement of Teaching.* Available online at http://archive.carnegiefoundation.org/pdfs/elibrary/Carnegie_Flexner_Report.pdf

[81] It is tempting to suspect these arguments were smokescreens, designed with some of the same cynicism and self-protection in mind as early standards for medical training. There's minimal evidence to support that contention, though. Even though there's not good science to support the idea that a doctoral degree or even a master's is required to be an effective therapist, psychologists appear to have been pursuing quality-of-care arguments in good faith.

[82] American Psychological Association (2014 April). Data blitz. *GradPSYCH, 12*(2), 7.

[83] Elchert, D. M. (2013). *Educating prospective students of professional psychology about the supply-demand internship crisis.* (No publisher location listed): Society for the Teaching of Psychology (APA Division 2). Available online at http://teachpsych.org/Resources/Documents/otrp/resources/elchert13.pdf

[84] Keilin. B. (2011 November). 2011 APPIC Match: Survey of internship applicants. *APPIC E-Newsletter*, November 2011, (pp. 8, 22-35). Available online at http://appic.mysharepointonline.com/Shared%20Training%20Resources/Newsletters/appic_november2011.pdf

[85] This is, admittedly, anecdotal data from those who have willingly shared their salaries at http://www.glassdoor.com/Salaries/psychology-postdoctoral-fellow-salary-SRCH_KO0,30.htm

[86] US Department of Labor, Wage and Hour Division (2010). Fact sheet #71: Internship programs under the Fair Labor Standards Act. Available online at http://www.dol.gov/whd/regs/compliance/whdfs71.pdf

[87] The differences largely depend on whether the nonprofit can be considered a "commercial enterprise," a question that requires its own legal analysis. See Jensen, D. G. (2013 July/August). Are nonprofits "commercial enterprises?" *The Therapist* magazine. Available online at https://www.camft.org/COS/Resources/Attorney_Articles/Dave/Are_Nonprofits_Commercial_Enterprises.aspx

[88] Tran-Lien, A. (2015 May/June). Recent Labor Board ruling sets precedent for California internships. *The Therapist, 27*(3), 43-46. Available online at https://www.camft.org/COS/Resources/Attorney_Articles/Ann/ Labor_Board_Sets_Precedent_for_California_Internships.aspx

[89] Returning to the FinAid.org calculators, this assumes 30-year repayment and 5% interest. No fees are included in the calculation.

[90] From BLS data.

[91] O'Connor, S. T. (2006). *Why don't they get licensed? Investigating success in the California Clinical Social Worker and Marriage and Family Therapist licensing process* (Master's thesis, California State University, Sacramento). Retrieved from http://www.csus.edu/ppa/thesis-project/bank/2010/OConnor.pdf

[92] Carrell, S. E., & West, J. E. (2010). Does professor quality matter? Evidence from random assignment of students to professors. *Journal of Political Economy, 118*(3), 409-432. Available online at http://www.econ.ucdavis.edu/faculty/scarrell/profqual2.pdf

[93] Hildebrandt, C. (2009). *Marriage and family therapy interns' best and worst supervision experiences* (Doctoral dissertation, Alliant International University).

[94] Anderson, S. A., Schlossberg, M., & Rigazio-DiGilio, S. (2000). Family therapy trainees' evaluation of their best and worst supervision experiences. *Journal of Marital and Family Therapy, 26*(1), 79-91.

[95] Lizzio, A., Wilson, K., & Que, J. (2009). Relationship dimensions in the professional supervision of psychology graduates: supervisee perceptions of processes and outcome. *Studies in Continuing Education, 31*(2), 127-140.

[96] Reichelt, S., & Skjerve, J. (2000). Supervision of inexperienced therapists: A qualitative analysis. *The Clinical Supervisor, 19*(2), 25-43.

[97] This assumption is so strong that many studies of supervision look at only alliance and satisfaction measures, without even assessing client outcomes. For example, in a structured review of 18 studies of how supervision impacts supervisees, *only one* included a meaningful measure of client outcome. See Wheeler, S., & Richards, K. (2007). The impact of clinical supervision on counsellors and therapists, their practice and their clients: A systematic review of the literature. *Counselling and Psychotherapy Research, 7*(1), 54-65.

[98] Miller, S. D., Hubble, M. A., Chow, D. L., & Seidel, J. A. (2013). The outcome of psychotherapy: Yesterday, today, and tomorrow. *Psychotherapy, 50*(1), 88-97.

[99] This commentary offers a good summary of supervision literature, addressing a wide variety of elements of the supervisory process and relationship. Note that almost every cited study defines effectiveness based on what supervisees liked, and that the skill development of the supervisee is barely mentioned, even by implication. That's not a criticism of the author, it's just a reflection on the current status of supervision practice and the related literature. Barnett, J. E. (2007). In search of the effective supervisor. *Professional Psychology: Research and Practice, 38*(3), 268-275.

[100] A couple of examples from the literature (there are many more): Kerl, S. B., Garcia, J. L., McCullough, C. S., & Maxwell, M. E. (2002). Systematic evaluation of professional performance: Legally supported procedure and process. *Counselor Education and Supervision, 41*(3), 321–332. Russell, C. S., DuPree, W. J., Beggs, M. A., Peterson, C. M., & Anderson, M. P. (2007). Responding to remediation and gatekeeping challenges in supervision. *Jorunal of Marital and Family Therapy, 33*(2), 227-244.

[101] California is the only state in the US that does not use the National MFT Exam; the structure and content of the state's MFT Standard Written Exam and MFT Written Clinical Exam, when combined, closely parallel the structure and content of the national exam.

[102] The graph is imperfect in other ways too; by looking at a single exam cycle, we're not really looking at a single group of examinees and how they progress. The best way to do that would be with an anonymized data set, one of which the BBS released in 2008. I've done the chart this way because it uses more recent data. The idea is the same, and the chart would be similar in either case; overwhelmingly those who stay in the exam process pass eventually. In the spring 2013 data as shown here, each shade represents those who pass at a particular number of attempts; the remaining area to the right of that shade is the proportion of those who failed the same attempt. Specific numbers are in the body text.

[103] Association of State and Provincial Psychology Boards (2012). 2012 psychology licensing exam scores by doctoral program. Peachtree City, GA: ASPPB. Available online at http://c.ymcdn.com/sites/www.asppb.net/resource/resmgr/EPPP_/2012_ASPPB_Exam_Scores_by_Do.pdf . Bear in mind that the 74% number reflects exam *attempts* passed, and not the per-

centage of *examinees* who pass. Someone who attempted three times, passing on the third attempt, would have all three attempts counted here. It is safe to say that the percentage of *examinees* who ultimately pass is well above 74%.

[104] Association of Social Work Boards (2015). *Pass rates*. Available online at https://www.aswb.org/exam-candidates/about-the-exams/pass-rates/

[105] NBCC doesn't actually post their pass rates, but this information comes from public documentation of California's deliberations around using national exams for LPCC licensure. This data also reflects the National Counselor Exam (NCE); the National Clinical Mental Health Counseling Exam (NCMHCE) pass rates are a bit lower, typically in the 60s-70s overall. For more on this, see http://www.bbs.ca.gov/pdf/agen_notice/2011/0311_licexam_material_v1.pdf . You'll also notice I left the National MFT Exam out of this discussion; AMFTRB, which administers the exam, doesn't appear to report overall pass rates. But based on the self-reporting of accredited programs, the pass rate seems to be quite high, perhaps above 90%: https://dx5br1z4f6n0k.cloudfront.net/iMIS15/Documents/COAMFTE/SAC%20Data/2014_National%20Exam%20Pass%20Rate%20(Full-time%20cohorts).pdf .

[106] See Angrist, J. D., & Guryan, J. (2008). Does teacher testing raise teacher quality? Evidence from state certification requirements. *Economics of Education Review, 27*(5), 483-503; Arathuzik, D. & Aber, C. (1998). Factors associated with national council licensure examination-registered nurse success. *Journal of Professional Nursing, 14*(2), 119-126.

[107] U.S. Department of Health and Human Services, Substance Abuse and Mental Health Services Administration (2013). *Report to Congress on the nation's substance abuse and mental health workforce issues.* Washington, DC: SAMHSA. Available online at https://store.samhsa.gov/shin/content/PEP13-RTC-BHWORK/PEP13-RTC-BHWORK.pdf . U.S. Department of Health and Human Services (2001). *Mental health: Culture, race, and ethnicity – A supplement to Mental health: A report of the Surgeon General.* Rockville, MD: SAMHSA. Available online at http://www.ncbi.nlm.nih.gov/books/NBK44243/

[108] As one example, see Friedman, R. A. (2015 July 17). Psychiatry's identity crisis. *The New York Times.* Available online at

http://www.nytimes.com/2015/07/19/opinion/psychiatrys-identity-crisis.html

[109] Ericsson, K. A. (2006). The influence of experience and deliberate practice on the development of superior expert performance. In K. A. Ericsson, N. Charness, R. R. Hoffman, & P. J. Feltovich (Eds.), *The Cambridge Handbook of Expertise and Expert Performance*, pp. 683-704. New York: Cambridge University Press.

[110] I highly recommend Miller's work and the ironically-named *Handbook* from the previous note, as each discusses the activities that *do* improve outcomes – things like deliberate practice and the purposeful solicitation of feedback. Common supervision tasks today (and to be fair, very little research has been done to determine what tasks supervisors actually do in supervision) bear little resemblance to what research shows would likely improve clinical outcomes.

[111] Okiishi, J. C., Lambert, M. J., Eggett, D., Nielsen, L., Dayton, D. D., & Vermeersch, D. A. (2006). An analysis of therapist treatment effects: Toward providing feedback to individual therapists on their clients' psychotherapy outcome. *Journal of Clinical Psychology, 62*(9), 1157-1172. We'll discuss this in greater detail in Task 4.

[112] APA. The quote comes from a sample letter they did in hopes that Psychologists would address the problem with legislators. http://www.apa.org/careers/early-career/sample-letter.pdf

[113] In the interest of full disclosure, I've been involved in this work through my volunteer role with AAMFT-California. I wrote AAMFT-CA's white paper on the current problems with MFT licensing in the state.

[114] Caldwell, B. E. (2013). *California family therapy program rankings: 34 of the state's best MFT programs*. Los Angeles, CA: Author.

[115] Baum, S., & Lapovsky, L. (2006). *Tuition discounting: Not just a private college practice*. New York: The College Board. Available online at http://www.collegeboard.com/prod_downloads/press/tuition-discounting.pdf

[116] You may understandably argue here that if all clinics paid their interns, then some clinics would not be able to gather the grant and donation money needed to keep their doors open, and the availability of no-cost and ultra-low-cost therapy for clients in difficult financial circumstances would decline. I agree that's probably true. I just can't find moral high ground in exploiting interns to make that kind of care available, especially given the increases in access to care described in the Introduction chapter. Many of

the clients who are going to no-cost and ultra-low-cost mental health clinics would qualify for subsidized health insurance that includes mental health coverage.
[117] Many of the arguments that psychology should move away from the pursuit of hard scientific knowledge come from two camps: Postmodernism (which is discussed later in this chapter) and the psychoanalytic community. Psychoanalysts often argue that the therapeutic process is best understood as art, since objective scientific knowledge will never supplant the role of the clinician's understanding of the suffering of the patient immediately in front of him or her. Whether you agree with that argument or not, the depictions of psychoanalytic therapy and the therapist in Sheldon Roth's *Psychotherapy: The art of wooing nature* (1987, Jason Aronson Inc.) are warm and empathetic, even poetic in nature. It's an impressive work.
[118] Duncan, B. L., Miller, S. D., Wampold, B. E., & Hubble, M. A. (2010). *The Heart and Soul of Change: Delivering What Works in Therapy (2nd ed.)*. Washington, DC: APA.
[119] For a brief overview of the philosophical differences at issue, see: Hoffman, L. (2005). Existential topics: Is psychotherapy an art or a science? Available online at http://www.existential-therapy.com/existential_topics/art_or_science.htm . Obviously, there are far more detailed works readily available on the underlying philosophies.
[120] http://www.apa.org/ed/about/reports/semi-january-2014.pdf
[121] Their definition of counseling is at http://www.counseling.org/knowledge-center/20-20-a-vision-for-the-future-of-counseling/consensus-definition-of-counseling, and their mission is at http://www.counseling.org/about-us/about-aca/our-mission
[122] Each of the codes is available online at the organization's web site.
APA: http://www.apa.org/ethics/code/index.aspx
ACA: http://www.counseling.org/Resources/aca-code-of-ethics.pdf
AAMFT: http://www.aamft.org/imis15/content/legal_ethics/code_of_ethics.aspx
NASW: http://www.socialworkers.org/pubs/code/code.asp
[123] Schwarz, A., & Cohen, S. (2013 March 31). ADHD seen in 11% of US children as diagnoses rise. *The New York Times.*
[124] DeSantis, A. D., Webb, E. M., & Noar, S. M. (2008). Illicit use of prescription ADHD medications on a college campus: A multimethodological approach. *Journal of American College Health, 57*(3), 315-323. Take

this with a big grain of salt because of selection bias and other methodological issues, but in this study, *more than one-third* of college students reported using ADHD medications without a prescription, and they described the process of getting those medications as easy and stigma-free.
[125] I'm usually loathe to cite WebMD when it can be avoided, but this is the best rundown of studies linking ADHD in childhood with adolescent and adult substance abuse. Note that these findings remain controversial, as other large-scale studies have not found such a link. http://www.webmd.com/add-adhd/guide/adhd-and-substance-abuse-is-there-a-link
[126] Conrad, P., & Bergey, M. R. (2014). The impending globalization of ADHD: Notes on the expansion and growth of a medicalized disorder. *Social Science and Medicine, 122*(1), 31-43.
[127] Singh, M. K., DelBello, M. P., Kowatch, R. A., & Strakowski, S. M. (2006). Co-occurrence of bipolar and attention-deficit hyperactivity disorders in children. *Bipolar Disorders, 8*(6), 710-720.
[128] Kutcher, S., Aman, M., Brooks, S. J., Buitelaar, J., van Daalen, E., Fegert, J., et al. (2004) International consensus statement on attention-deficit/hyperactivity disorder (ADHD) and disruptive behaviour disorders (DBDs): clinical implications and treatment practice suggestions. *European Journal of Neuropsychopharmacology, 14*(1), 11-28.
[129] Guilé, J. M., & Greenfield, B. (2004). Introduction: Personality disorders in childhood and adolescence. *Canadian Child and Adolescent Psychiatry Review, 13*(3), 51-52.
[130] Webb, A. R., & Speer, J. R. (1986). Prototype of a profession: Psychology's public image. *Professional Psychology: Research and Practice, 17*(1), 5-9.
[131] Allen Frances' 2013 book *Saving Normal* (HarperCollins) has a thorough detailing of the satanic ritual abuse diagnostic fad and other historical diagnostic fads in mental health, going back centuries.
[132] Munro, D. (2015 April 27). Inside the $35 billion addiction treatment industry. *Forbes.* Available online at http://www.forbes.com/sites/danmunro/2015/04/27/inside-the-35-billion-addiction-treatment-industry/
[133] While the anonymous structure of AA has in some cases made research difficult, there is a wealth of data comparing different kinds of treatment (including AA and related 12-step programs). Specific to alcohol

abuse, the best current estimates put the success rate of AA somewhere between 5 and 10 percent.

[134] Hester, R. K., & Miller, W. R. (2002). *Handbook of alcoholism treatment approaches: Effective alternatives (3rd ed.)*. Boston: Allyn and Bacon.

[135] It's a bit afield here, but for a brain-based argument against the disease model of addiction, you might also be interested in Lewis, M. (2015). *The Biology of Desire: Why Addiction Is Not a Disease*. Philadelphia, PA: Perseus Books.

[136] The bill was California Senate Bill 570, visible here: http://leginfo.legislature.ca.gov/faces/billTextClient.xhtml?bill_id=2013201 40SB570 . The limitation in scope to solely abstinence-based approaches is in section 4454(c)(2)(D). For a review of the much more effective harm-reduction based approaches, see Hester, R. K., & Miller, W. R. (2002). *Handbook of alcoholism treatment approaches: Effective alternatives (3rd ed.)*. Boston: Allyn and Bacon.

[137] Munro, D. (2015 April 27). Inside the $35 billion addiction treatment industry. *Forbes*. Available online at http://www.forbes.com/sites/danmunro/2015/04/27/inside-the-35-billion-addiction-treatment-industry/

[138] Neill, J. (1990). Whatever became of the schizophrenogenic mother? *American Journal of Psychotherapy, 44*(4), 499-505.

[139] Whitaker, R. (2008). *Mad in America: Bad science, bad medicine, and the enduring mistreatment of the mentally ill*. New York: Basic Books.

[140] Kuipers, E. (2006). Family interventions in schizophrenia: Evidence for efficacy and proposed mechanisms of change. *Journal of Family Therapy, 28*(1), 73–80.

[141] Lilienfeld, S. O. (2012). Public skepticism of psychology: Why many people perceive the study of human behavior as unscientific. *American Psychologist, 67*(2), 111-129.

[142] You may rightly wonder whether I engaged in the shenanigans of p-hacking and small sample size noted above. I did my best not to. I had a sample of more than 200 licensed MFTs in California, and while I did assess dozens of variables (participants completed an attitudes-toward-marriage scale, the myths questionnaire, and a demographic questionnaire), I reduced alpha to 0.01 when doing the individual item analyses to greatly reduce the risk of false positives. Even then, where positive results did show up, they

were framed carefully to acknowledge the risk that they could have just been random noise. My dissertation went on to win the 2005 AAMFT Dissertation Award.

[143] While several studies support these conclusions, one of the strongest recent studies on the topic is Aughinbaugh, A., Robles, O., & Sun, H. (2013 October). Marriage and divorce: Patterns by gender, race, and educational attainment. *Monthly Labor Review*. Available online at http://www.bls.gov/opub/mlr/2013/article/pdf/marriage-and-divorce-patterns-by-gender-race-and-educational-attainment.pdf

[144] Rampage, C. (2002). Marriage in the 20th century: A feminist perspective. *Family Process, 41*(2), 261-268.

[145] These studies do generally attempt to account for the under-reporting of intimate partner violence, if you're wondering. For the US: Tjaden, P., & Thoennes, N. (2000). *Full report of the prevalence, incidence, and consequences of violence against women.* Washington, DC: National Institute of Justice and Centers for Disease Control and Prevention. For Canada: Federal/Provincial/Territorial Ministers Responsible for the Status of Women (2002). *Assessing violence against women: A statistical profile.* Canada: Author. For Australia: Coumarelos, C., & Allen, J. (1998). *Predicting violence against women: The 1996 women's safety survey.* New South Wales, Australia: Bureau of Crime Statistics and Research.

[146] Larson, J. H. (1988). The marriage quiz: College students' beliefs in selected myths about marriage. *Family Relations, 37*(1), 3-11.

[147] Ægisdóttir, S., White, M. J., Spengler, P. M., Maugherman, A. S., Anderson, L. A., Cook, R. S., et al. (2006). The Meta-Analysis of Clinical Judgment Project: Fifty-six years of accumulated research on clinical versus statistical prediction. *The Counseling Psychologist, 34*(3), 341-382.

[148] Meehl, P. E. (1956). Symposium on clinical and statistical prediction: The tie that binds. *Journal of Counseling Psychology, 3*(3), 163–164.

[149] Freedman, L. P., Cockburn, I. M., & Simcoe, T. S. (2015). The economics of reproducibility in clinical research. *PLoS Biology, 13*(6), e1002165. Available online at http://journals.plos.org/plosbiology/article?id=10.1371/journal.pbio.1002165

[150] Fanelli, D. (2010). "Positive" results increase down the hierarchy of the sciences. *PLoS ONE 5*(4), e10068. Available online at http://journals.plos.org/plosone/article?id=10.1371/journal.pone.0010068

[151] The whole story of how and why Bohannon did this, along with an explanation for how measuring 18 variables makes it likely that at least one will give a positive result, is in Bohannon's own recounting of the story: Bohannon, J. (2015 May 27). I fooled millions into thinking chocolate helps weight loss. Here's how. *Io9*. Available online at http://io9.com/i-fooled-millions-into-thinking-chocolate-helps-weight-1707251800

[152] Cacioppo, J. T., Cacioppo, S., Gonzaga, G. C., Ogburn, E. L., & VanderWeele, T. J. (2013 June 18). Marital satisfaction and break-ups differ across on-line and off-line meeting venues. *PNAS, 110*(25), 10135-10140. Available online at http://www.pnas.org/content/110/25/10135.full.pdf

[153] Ioannidis, J. P. A. (2005). Why most published research findings are false. *PLOS Medicine, 2*(8), e124. Available online at http://journals.plos.org/plosmedicine/article?id=10.1371/journal.pmed.0020 124 . It should be added that Ioannidis is hardly the only researcher to come to this conclusion; it's not even terribly controversial. Many researchers and research institutions are currently focused not on challenging this conclusion but on developing ways to ensure greater reliability of findings, such as requiring researchers to submit hypotheses *before* they conduct their research so as to avoid HARKing.

[154] This is a surprisingly complex area of research – good in that lots of people are exploring it in different ways, and challenging in that the results often only suggest more complexity. To get a feel for where this literature stands, check out the literature review in Bhati, K. S. (2014). Effect of client-therapist gender match on the therapeutic relationship: An exploratory analysis. *Psychological Reports: Relationships & Communications, 115*(2), 565-583.

[155] For a fairly recent meta-analysis of clinical judgment versus actuarial (statistical) judgment in psychotherapy, see Aegisdottir, S., White, M. J., Spengler, P. M., Maugherman, A. S., Anderson, L. A., Cook, R. S., et al. (2006). The meta-analysis of clinical judgment project: Fifty-six years of accumulated research on clinical versus statistical prediction. *The Counseling Psychologist, 34*(3), 341-382. For a somewhat broader examination of clinical versus actuarial judgment in mental health care, see Grove, W. M., Zald, D. H., Lebow, B. S., Snitz, B. E., & Nelson, C. (2000). Clinical vs. mechanical prediction: A meta-analysis. *Psychological Assessment, 12*(1), 19-30.

[156] It's easy to quibble with the conceptualization of "waves" here, as there are several competing ideas about what forms of therapy constitute a "wave" in an ever-evolving field. I join those who think of psychoanalysis as the first wave of psychotherapy, behavioral and cognitive approaches as the second wave, and postmodern approaches as the third. But this is debatable. For a good history of the development of postmodern approaches in therapy, I would recommend Anderson, H. (1997). *Conversation, language, and possibilities: A postmodern approach to therapy.* New York: Basic Books. For a helpful and highly intellectual discussion of the benefits of postmodernism to the discourse in psychological science, have a go at Gergen, K. J. (2001). Psychological science in a postmodern context. *American Psychologist, 56*(10), 803-813.

[157] Summarized here from Anderson, H. (1997). *Conversation, language, and possibilities: A postmodern approach to therapy.* New York: Basic Books.

[158] I'm just talking about counseling or therapy itself here. To be sure, there is a much more sordid history when it comes to psychological *research* with oppressed populations, the scars of which are long-lasting. Those who identify as African-American, LGBT, or as one of several other groups cruelly "studied" by psychologists and other mental health professionals have good reason to be skeptical when we offer our "help."

[159] There's an excellent and detailed explanation of why postmodernists reject core scientific assumptions in Ashworth, P. (2008). Conceptual foundations of qualitative psychology. In J. A. Smith (Ed.), *Qualitative psychology: A practical guide to research methods (2nd ed.)*, pp. 4-25. Thousand Oaks, CA: Sage. It's pro-research but anti-science, at least as it relates to studying human experience and behavior.

[160] It's worth adding here that postmodernists do express concern about the power inherent in holding "knowledge" that others lack – so much so that postmodernists consider knowledge and power inseperable. See Sanders, C. J. (2011). An exploration of knowledge and power in narrative, collaborative-based, postmodern therapies: A commentary. *The Professional Counselor, 1*(3), 201-207. Available online at http://tpcjournal.nbcc.org/wp-content/uploads/2014/09/pages-201-207-sanders.pdf

[161] Greene, J. C. (2007). *Mixed methods in social inquiry.* San Francisco, CA: Jossey-Bass.

[162] Multiple postmodern scholars have tried to push back against this misunderstanding of postmodern principles, including Anderson, H. (1997). *Conversation, language, and possibilities: A postmodern approach to therapy.* New York: Basic Books. Rober, P. (2002). Constructive hypothesizing, dialogic understanding and the therapist's inner conversation: Some ideas about knowing and not knowing in the family therapy session. *Journal of Marital and Family Therapy, 28*(4), 467-478.

[163] There are many examples of this in the literature, but here are two that are particularly clear: Addis, M. E., & Krasnow, A. D. (2000). A national survey of practicing psychologists' attitudes toward psychotherapy treatment manuals. *Journal of Consulting and Clinical Psychology, 68*(2), 331-339. Borntrager, C. F., Chorpita, B. F., Higa-McMillan, C., & Weisz, J. R. (2009). Provider attitudes toward evidence-based practices: Are the concerns with the evidence or the manuals? *Psychiatric Services, 60*(5), 677-681.

[164] Los Angeles County Department of Mental Health (2011). *Prevention and early intervention: Evidence-based practices, promising practices, and community-defined evidence practices: Resource guide 2.0.* Los Angeles, CA: Author. Available online at http://file.lacounty.gov/dmh/cms1_159575.pdf

[165] Borntrager, C. F., Chorpita, B. F., Higa-McMillan, C., & Weisz, J. R. (2009). Provider attitudes toward evidence-based practices: Are the concerns with the evidence or the manuals? *Psychiatric Services, 60*(5), 677-681.

[166] Johnson, S. M. (2004). *Creating connection: The practice of emotionally focused therapy (2ⁿᵈ ed.).* New York: Brunner/Routledge. This particular quote appears on page 55.

[167] I find this stuff fascinating, so feel free to follow me down the rabbit hole. Eliza is perhaps the best-known (and least-sophisticated) example of an artificial therapist; you can play with an Eliza bot at http://www.manifestation.com/neurotoys/eliza.php3 . More recently, a virtual, animated weight-loss coach helped people reach their goals more effectively than those without the coach – speaking directly to the relational piece, those who had the coach reported feeling guilt if they skipped an appointment. Read about that study here: http://www.healthcareitnews.com/news/virtual-coaches-keep-overweight-people-track . Specific to mental health, there are several iterations of artifi-

cial "therapy bots" under development; one of the developers discusses how these virtual professionals can be useful here: https://www.psychologytoday.com/blog/mind-tapas/201306/my-psychiatrist-is-robot

[168] Hubble, M. A., Duncan, B. L., Miller, S. D., & Wampold, B. E. (2010). Introduction. In B. L. Duncan, S. D. Miller, B. E. Wampold, & M. A. Hubble (Eds.), *The Heart and Soul of Change: Delivering What Works in Therapy (2nd ed.)*, pp 23-46. Washington, DC: APA.

[169] Webb, A. R., & Speer, J. R. (1986). Prototype of a profession: Psychology's public image. *Professional Psychology: Research and Practice, 17*(1), 5-9.

Also: Hartwig, S. G., & Delin, C. (2003). How unpopular are we? Reassessing psychologists' public image with different measures of favourability. *Australian Psychologist, 38*(1), 68-72.

[170] These are summarized from Cozolino, L. (2010). *The neuroscience of psychotherapy: Healing the social brain (2nd ed.)*. New York: W. W. Norton & Co.

[171] This quote is from page 161 of Cozolino's text.

[172] Levitt, S. D., & Dubner, S. J. (2009). *Super freakonomics: Global cooling, patriotic prostitutes and why suicide bombers should buy life insurance.* New York: HarperCollins. This quote is from page 13.

[173] These findings are all retold in Levitt, S. D., & Dubner, S. J. (2005). *Freakonomics: A rogue economist explores the hidden side of everything.* New York: William Morrow. In each case, there's a meaningful counterargument to be made, and Levitt & Dubner are simply describing the work of other economists. Nonetheless, the findings they describe are compelling, and demonstrate just how far behavioral economics has come in answering questions that are fundamental to the work of changing human behavior.

[174] This and the following paragraph reflect the "marital discord" model of depression, researched most prolifically by Steven Beach. The research findings on this one question come from O'Leary, K. D., Risso, L. P., & Beach, S. R. H. (1990). Attributions about the marital discord/depression link and therapy outcome. *Behavior Therapy, 21*(4), 413–422.

[175] Wang, P. S., Lane, M., Olfson, M., Pincus, H. A., Wells, K. B., & Kessler, R. C. (2005) Twelve-month use of mental health services in the United States: Results from the National Comorbidity Survey Replication. *Archives of General Psychiatry, 62*(6), 629-640.

[176] Walach, H., & Kirsch, I. (2015). Herbal treatments and antidepressant medication: Similar data, divergent conclusions. In S. O. Lilienfeld, S. J. Lynn, & J. M. Lohr (Eds.), *Science and Pseudoscience in Clinical Psychology (2nd ed.)*, pp. 364-390. New York: Guilford Press. This quote is from page 380-381. The "Rather than..." quote a couple of paragraphs above comes from page 380.

[177] From this fascinating 2009 story in *Wired* magazine: Silberman, S. (2009 August 24). Placebos are getting more effective. Drugmakers are desperate to know why. *Wired*. Available online at http://archive.wired.com/medtech/drugs/magazine/17-09/ff_placebo_effect?currentPage=all

[178] Fournier, J. C., DeRubeis, R. J., Hollon, S. D., Dimidjian, S., Amsterdam, J. D., Shelton, R. C., et al. (2010). Antidepressant drug effects and depression severity: A patient-level meta-analysis. *JAMA, 303*(1), 47-53.

[179] Johnsen, T. J., & Friborg, O. (2015). The effects of cognitive behavioral therapy as an anti-depressive treatment is falling: A meta-analysis. *Psychological Bulletin, 141*(4), 747-768.

[180] Harris Interactive (2008 July 2). *Mental health treatment: It's commonly accepted yet not so easy to obtain or understand*. Available online at http://www.harrisinteractive.com/vault/Harris_Interactive_News_2008_07_02.pdf

[181] Ensuring adequate privacy and confidentiality of these recordings is a major concern for clinicians and researchers alike. Both federal law and professional ethics codes offer some flexibility in what would be considered appropriate steps to protecting the security of these recordings, and it's an area of technological advancement in health care that could be a whole book unto itself. For our purposes, it will suffice to say that part of the ongoing improvement in these technologies is improvement in the secure storage of recordings.

[182] Patterson, J. E., Miller, R. B., Carnes, S., & Wilson, S. (2004). Evidence-based practice for marriage and family therapists. *Journal of Marital and Family Therapy, 30*(2), 183-195. This quote appears on page 184.

[183] Summarized from Hubble, M. A., Duncan, B. L., Miller, S. D., & Wampold, B. E. (2010). Introduction. In B. L. Duncan, S. D. Miller, B. E. Wampold, & M. A. Hubble (Eds.), *The Heart and Soul of Change: Delivering What Works in Therapy (2nd ed.)*, pp 23-46. Washington, DC: APA.

[184] Henriksen, C. A., Stein, M. B., Afifi, T. O., Enns, M. W., Lix, L. M., & Sareen, J. (2015). Identifying factors that predict longitudinal outcomes of untreated common mental disorders. *Psychiatric Services, 66*(2), 163-170.

[185] Summarized from Hubble, M. A., Duncan, B. L., Miller, S. D., & Wampold, B. E. (2010). Introduction. In B. L. Duncan, S. D. Miller, B. E. Wampold, & M. A. Hubble (Eds.), *The Heart and Soul of Change: Delivering What Works in Therapy (2nd ed.)*, pp 23-46. Washington, DC: APA. The next paragraph is also summarized from this text, excepting the piece about therapist biases that is separately referenced.

[186] There are lots of references that could be offered for each of these factors and more, so consider these examples. Garb, H. N. (1997). Race bias, social class bias, and gender bias in clinical judgment. *Clinical Psychology: Science and Practice, 4*(2), 99–120. Specifically on weight: Davis-Coelho, K., Waltz, J., & Davis-Coelho, B. (2000). Awareness and prevention of bias against fat clients in psychotherapy. *Professional Psychology: Research and Practice, 31*(6), 682–684.

[187] Sprenkle, D. H., Davis, S. D., & Lebow, J. L. (2009). *Common factors in couple and family therapy: The overlooked foundation for effective practice*. New York: Guilford Press. This specific quote appears on page 61. The maps metaphor I use in the next paragraph also owes a debt to this text, which refers to models as roadmaps and common factors as the driving forces behind therapeutic change.

[188] Okiishi, J. C., Lambert, M. J., Eggett, D., Nielsen, L., Dayton, D. D., & Vermeersch, D. A. (2006). An analysis of therapist treatment effects: Toward providing feedback to individual therapists on their clients' psychotherapy outcome. *Journal of Clinical Psychology, 62*(9), 1157-1172.

[189] Miller, S., Hubble, M., & Duncan, B. (no date). The secrets of supershrinks: Pathways to clinical excellence. *Psychotherapy Networker Clinical Reports.* Available online at http://www.scottdmiller.com/wp-content/uploads/2014/06/Supershrinks-Free-Report-1.pdf

[190] Miller, S., & Hubble, M. (2011 May/June). The road to mastery. *Psychotherapy Networker, 35*(3), 22-31, 60. Available online at http://scottdmiller.com/wp-content/uploads/The%20Road%20to%20Mastery.PDF

[191] Courts don't take cases of ineffective treatment: Leslie, R. S. (2014 January). Alphabet soup for the new year. *CPH & Associates Avoiding Lia-*

*bility Bulletin.* Available online at
http://www.cphins.com/legalresources/bulletin/avoiding-liability . Courts
don't move unlawful-termination cases forward when there is clear documentation: Muller, D. (2008). *The right things to do to avoid wrongful
termination claims.* Available online at
http://www.workforce.com/articles/the-right-things-to-do-to-avoid-
wrongful-termination-claims

[192] The stances taken on reparative or conversion therapy by many
medical and mental health professional associations are nicely gathered and
summarized here: http://www.hrc.org/resources/entry/policy-and-position-
statements-on-conversion-therapy

[193] This struggle is addressed well in the book *Science and Pseudoscience in Clinical Psychology* (Guilford, 2015), which belongs on your
bookshelf.

[194] Forrest, L. M. (2012). *Ethics Committee: 2011 annual report.*
Available online at http://www.apa.org/about/governance/bdcmte/2011-
ethics.aspx

[195] Pope, K. S., Tabachnick, B. G., & Kieth-Spiegel, P. (1987). Ethics
of practice: The beliefs and behaviors of psychologists as therapists. *American Psychologist, 42*(11), 993-1006. Available online at
http://kspope.com/ethics/research4.php

[196] Riemersma, M. (2010 July/August). The typical California MFT.
*The Therapist, 22*(4). Available online at
https://www.camft.org/COS/Resources/Attorney_Articles/Mary/The_Typica
l_California_MFT_2010.aspx

[197] Pope, K. S. (2001). Sex between therapists and clients. In J. Worrell
(Ed.), *Encyclopedia of Women and Gender: Sex similarities and differences
and the impact of society on gender, Vol. 2*, pp. 955-962. Available online at
http://www.kspope.com/sexiss/sexencyc.php . It's worth noting here that
while this certainly still happens, the percentage of therapists who admit to
sexual relationships with clients has declined markedly since the 1970s,
when more than 10% of psychologists acknowledged having had such relationships. Of course, as with any stigmatized behavior, it is hard to know
whether the declines seen in survey data reflect an actual decline in therapists *having* sexual relationships with clients, or whether they instead reflect
a decline in therapists *willing to admit* they have had sexual relationships
with clients.

[198] Pope, K. S., & Vetter, V. A. (1992). Ethical dilemmas encountered by members of the American Psychological Association: A national survey. *American Psychologist, 47*(3), 397-411. Available online at http://www.kspope.com/ethics/ethics2.php

[199] Of those, 643 were received by the Board of Psychology and 1,243 by the Board of Behavioral Sciences (S. Sodergren, personal communication, August 4, 2015).

[200] Of those 133, 29 were issued by the Board of Psychology (as posted to their web site), 104 by the Board of Behavioral Sciences (S. Sodergren, personal communication, August 4, 2015).

[201] Board of Behavioral Sciences (2014). Supplemental materials for the November 19-20, 2014 meeting of the Board of Behavioral Sciences. Sacramento, CA: BBS. Available online at http://www.bbs.ca.gov/pdf/agen_notice/2014/1114_bdmtg_suppmaterial.pdf . The relevant data here is on page 20, in the row "Average days to complete" under "Disciplinary orders."

[202] Bernard, J. L., & Jara, C. S. (1986). The failure of clinical psychology graduate students to apply understood ethical principles. *Professional Psychology: Research and Practice, 17*(4), 313-315.

[203] These schemes don't always work as well as hoped. One evaluation of a scoring scheme test-driven in Oregon found that when physicians were categorized among the least efficient in a single year, there was more than a 50% chance that they would not fall into the same category the next year, even when the scoring was done retrospectively so the doctors couldn't have been meaningfully changing their practices. http://www.cms.gov/Research-Statistics-Data-and-Systems/Statistics-Trends-and-Reports/Reports/downloads/StabilityinPhysicianScores_2010.pdf

[204] Fox, S., & Duggan, M. (2013). *Health Online 2013.* Washington, DC: Pew Research Center's Internet and American Life Project. Available online at http://bibliobase.sermais.pt:8008/BiblioNET/Upload/PDF5/003820.pdf

[205] Weber, R. L. (2013 October 10). The travel agent is dying, but it's not dead yet. *CNN.* Available online at http://www.cnn.com/2013/10/03/travel/travel-agent-survival/

[206] Hubble, M. A., Duncan, B. L., & Miller, S. D. (1999). *The heart and soul of change: What works in therapy.* Washington, DC: APA.

[207] I don't give this concern a lot of weight, for reasons I covered in the Introduction, but it is a concern among many. See Hubble, M. A., Duncan, B. L., Miller, S. D., & Wampold, B. E. (2010). Introduction. In B. L. Duncan, S. D. Miller, B. E. Wampold, & M. A. Hubble (Eds.), *The Heart and Soul of Change: Delivering What Works in Therapy (2nd ed.)*, pp 23-46. Washington, DC: APA.

[208] There are many examples of such exercises, but I'm particularly fond of the Objective Structured Clinical Exercise (OSCE) developed at the University of Oregon.

[209] Interestingly, Texas is an example of a state that requires some of their mental health licensees to retake the state jurisprudence exam every time they renew their license. The exam is done online from the licensee's own computer, and as such it is not terribly burdensome. It seems like a reasonable and efficient way to ensure that licensees are, at a minimum, maintaining awareness of the current legal requirements for their practices. That said, the jurisprudence exam is focused only on legal issues, and offers no evaluation of one's awareness of current clinical practices.

[210] If the SRS and ORS do suggest a need to get better, they aren't necessarily great at demonstrating *how* you need to get better. The SRS addresses issues of therapeutic alliance, and the ORS addresses issues of progress toward desired outcomes; what these measures can't say is what specific areas need improvement. So if a weakness is shown, I would encourage the use of more specific questionnaires, or consultation with a trusted colleague, to further define where you should focus your energy in professional development.

[211] The WHODAS is just one of a great many assessment measures that the American Psychiatric Association has made freely available online for clinicians to use in conjunction with the DSM-5. They're available at http://www.psychiatry.org/practice/dsm/dsm5/online-assessment-measures

[212] For more information, visit http://www.psychlops.org.uk/

[213] For more information, visit http://www.oqmeasures.com/measures/adult-measures/oq-45/

[214] Miller, S. D., Duncan, B. L., Brown, J., Sorrell, R., & Chalk, M. B. (2006). Using formal client feedback to improve retention and outcome: Making ongoing, real-time assessment feasible. *Journal of Brief Therapy, 5*(1), 5-22.

[215] Each of the codes is available online at the organization's web site.

· APA: http://www.apa.org/ethics/code/index.aspx
ACA: http://www.counseling.org/Resources/aca-code-of-ethics.pdf
AAMFT: http://www.aamft.org/imis15/content/legal_ethics/
code_of_ethics.aspx
NASW: http://www.socialworkers.org/pubs/code/code.asp

[216] California, for example, phrases the requirement this way: "A false, fraudulent, misleading, or deceptive statement, claim, or image includes a [...] scientific claim that cannot be substantiated by reliable, peer reviewed, published scientific studies" (California Business and Professions Code, section 651(b)(7)).

[217] This is also a problem in therapist education, though progress is slowly being made here. A combination of state laws and accreditation requirements are leading programs to be more transparent about cost, program length, and most importantly, student outcomes in such areas as licensure and employment. While some schools have resisted these efforts, we must trust that students and clients alike are rational decision-makers – they don't all choose based on the same criteria, but they do make choices based on the best information available to them.

[218] Miller, S., & Hubble, M. (2011 May/June). The road to mastery. *Psychotherapy Networker, 35*(3), 22-31, 60. Available online at http://scottdmiller.com/wp-content/uploads/The%20Road%20to%20Mastery.PDF

[219] Pew Research Center (2014). *Millennials in adulthood: Detached from institutions, networked with friends.* Available online at http://www.pewsocialtrends.org/files/2014/03/2014-03-07_generations-report-version-for-web.pdf

[220] Some researchers have cast a less-than-friendly light on this reality, noting that Millennials score higher than prior generations on measures of narcissism. Others argue that a focus on personal fulfillment and tangible rewards for behavior are natural results of having lived through a major economic recession. The debate is beyond the scope of this book, but a fascinating one.

[221] US Census Bureau data at http://www.census.gov/hhes/socdemo/education/data/cps/historical/fig11.jpg

[222] There are just over 100,000 licensed psychologists, according to the APA. This estimate is available online at http://www.apa.org/support/about/psych/numbers-us.aspx#answer

There are just over 400,000 licensed master's level therapists, according to the ACA. This estimate is available online at http://calpcc.org/mental-health-professions-statics-2013

The estimate of one therapist for roughly every 480 adults is based on comparing the numbers of therapists with an estimate of the total US adult population drawn from Census Bureau data at http://quickfacts.census.gov/qfd/states/00000.html

# About the Author

Benjamin E. Caldwell, PsyD, is an Associate Professor for the Couple and Family Therapy Graduate Programs at the California School of Professional Psychology at Alliant International University in Los Angeles. He specializes in legal, ethical, and policy issues in the mental health professions.